Studies in Writing & Rhetoric

Other Books in the Studies in Writing & Rhetoric Series

Mutuality in the Rhetoric and Composition Classroom

Mutuality in the Rhetoric and Composition Classroom

David L. Wallace and
Helen Rothschild Ewald

SOUTHERN ILLINOIS UNIVERSITY PRESS

Carbondale and Edwardsville

Publication partially funded by a subvention grant from The Conference on College Composition and Communication of the National Council of Teachers of English.

A previous version of chapter 4 appeared as "Exploring Agency in Classroom Discourse or Should David Have Told His Story?" in the October 1994 issue of *College Composition and Communication.* Copyright 1994 by the National Council of Teachers of English. Reprinted with permission.

Library of Congress Cataloging-in-Publication Data

Wallace, David L., 1960–
Mutuality in the rhetoric and composition classroom / David L. Wallace and Helen Rothschild Ewald.
p. cm.
Includes bibliographical references (p.) and index.
1. English language—Rhetoric—Study and teaching. 2. English language—Composition and exercises. 3. Teacher-student relationships. 4. Mutualism. I. Ewald, Helen Rothschild. II. Title.
ISBN 0-8093-2324-9 (alk. paper)
PE1404.W33 2000
808′.042′07—dc21   99-051750

*To the students and teachers
who have inspired us
to keep learning*

Contents

Preface

This book represents a seven-year journey in which we put moments from our teaching under a microscope, asked each other hard questions, shared successes, and commiserated over failures. This collaboration began as a mail-room conversation about the frustrations of trying to do something different in our classrooms and grew from a seemingly simple agreement to visit each other's classes into a research project, a *College Composition and Communication* article, and finally this book. Along the way, we learned a great deal about who we are as teachers and what we try to offer our students.

We intend this book as an invitation for others to take similar journeys in their teaching, not because we think everyone should reach the same destinations that we have but because the journey itself is what matters.

Acknowledgments

Work on this project was supported by a grant from the Provost's Office at Iowa State University. We are grateful for the support and contributions of many colleagues in the Department of English at Iowa State, including Nancy Blyler, Brenda Daly, Sheryl Kamps, Smokey McKinney, Walden Miller, and Sue Tatro. In addition, we gratefully acknowledge the advice of colleagues in the field at large who helped us shape this work into its current form: Glynda Hull, Kay M. Losey, Joseph Harris, Anne DiPardo, Nedra Reynolds, John Schilb, and particularly Robert Brooke.

We could not have completed this work without the support of our families. We thank Judy Gough for the many patient hours she spent transcribing tapes, and we thank Bob, James, and Jessica Ewald for their patience and for graciously fetching Helen to the phone each time David called for an impromptu consultation.

Finally, we acknowledge the great debt we owe the many teachers and students who have inspired us. Many of our teaching heroes who happen to be published pedagogical theorists are cited in this book, but there are many other past teachers, current colleagues, student teachers, and graduate teaching assistants whose classroom efforts informed the thinking that underlies this book but whose names do not appear in it. Also, the students who have let us use their work in this book represent thousands of others who have been our partners in our continual explorations of what it means to teach and learn. Their energy and commitment to learning draws us back to the classroom each fall.

Mutuality in the Rhetoric and Composition Classroom

1 / Toward Mutuality in the Classroom: Classroom Speech Genres, Course Architecture, and Interpretive Agency

> There is so close a connection between ideas and WORDS . . .
> that it is impossible to speak clearly and distinctly of our knowl-
> edge which all consists in propositions, without considering, first,
> the nature, use, and signification of Language.
>
> —John Locke,
> "An Essay Concerning Human Understanding"

> Human beings are not built in silence, but in word, in work, in
> action-reflection.
>
> —Paolo Freire,
> *Pedagogy of the Oppressed*

> Moving from silence into speech is for the oppressed, the colo-
> nized, the exploited, and those who stand and struggle side by
> side a gesture of defiance that heals, that makes new life and new
> growth possible. It is that act of speech, of "talking back," that is
> no mere gesture of empty words, that is the expression of our
> movement from object to subject—the liberated voice.
>
> —bell hooks,
> *Talking Back: Thinking Feminist, Thinking Black*

In the epigraphs above, Freire and hooks suggest that the intimacy
between thought and language that Locke acknowledges has important implications for education. Both Freire and hooks implicitly argue for the centrality of rhetoric in the academy, recognizing that
finding ways to speak is integrally bound up with the ability to take
action. Further, hooks argues that having a voice is critical for those
who have traditionally been silenced by dominant culture. The argument for the centrality of rhetoric in the academy matches an assumption that seems basic to classroom teaching: simply put, there

is an intimate connection between language and knowledge making. Although it may be common to assume this connection, it is equally common to underestimate the power of classroom language to both construct and reflect knowledge as well as social relations in the classroom. And, as we argue in this book, recognizing the constitutive nature of language is only the beginning of a pedagogy that invites students to take subject positions as co-constructors of knowledge. The impetus to engage in *alternative pedagogy* must be worked out in language—in discourse among teachers and students that transforms traditional classroom roles.[1]

Implicit in the preceding statement is the assumption that teacher and student roles are in need of change in today's classrooms. This need for change survives despite a considerable history of progressive (Deweyan), critical (Marxist), and feminist efforts to alter the types of knowledge making and the nature of the discourse relations in American education. These efforts, although essential to foregrounding difficulties in traditional educational approaches, have been criticized for reasons ranging from "weaknesses or shortcomings in the construction of 'empowerment'" (see Gore, "What" 54) to a defective ideological foundation: "key assumptions, goals, and pedagogical practices fundamental to the literature on critical pedagogy—namely, 'empowerment,' 'student voice,' 'dialogue,' and even the term 'critical'—are repressive myths that perpetuate relations of domination" (Ellsworth 91).

In the composition classroom, the irony and frustration of unsuccessful struggles to be alternative are epitomized in a classroom discourse study conducted by Glynda Hull, Mike Rose, Kay Losey Fraser, and Marisa Castellano. These researchers observed that even when a writing teacher was openly committed to the liberatory goal of student empowerment, she "inadvertently participate[d] in the social construction of attitudes and beliefs" that worked to reproduce traditional teacher-student relations, as well as to promote dominant class and race-based biases toward various types of discourse. Compounding this irony was that, in a classroom centered on language and rhetorical study, certain deeply rooted language practices, including traditional question-response-evaluation classroom discourse patterns, undermined the teacher's liberatory goals. In short, the impetus to empower students by engaging them in liberatory and emancipatory pedagogies is simply not enough.

The main purpose of this book is to help readers identify, theorize, and work through problems faced by teachers who already value alternative approaches but are still struggling to implement them in the classroom. This said, we do not imply that teachers must depend on theorists to articulate detailed classroom methodologies for effecting liberatory and emancipatory goals. Quite the reverse. We believe that teachers, through pedagogical practice within their individual classrooms, represent a powerful force capable of effecting many of the changes envisioned in alternative approaches.[2] As Roger I. Simon, in writing about Henry Giroux's "pedagogy of possibility," asserts, those seeking such pedagogies cannot depend on abstract, decontextualized visions of what these alternative forms might be like. Rather, those seeking these pedagogies must "approach such a task strategically, locally and contextually formulating practice within an integrated moral and epistemological stance" (58). And, we would add, those seeking to work within alternative pedagogies in the writing classroom must, in remapping authority and relations of power in the classroom, eventually address "how and whether academic discourse can be reconfigured so that it might go beyond simply inverting the hierarchy of authorized discourse types" (see Mortensen and Kirsch 569).

Defining Mutuality as a Key Factor in Alternative Pedagogy

At the heart of the change that has been variously envisioned by Deweyan, Marxist, and feminist approaches is the concept we call *mutuality*. When articulated as a classroom goal, mutuality can be understood as teachers and students sharing the potential to adopt a range of subject positions and to establish reciprocal discourse relations as they negotiate meaning in the classroom. Identifying mutuality as a key factor in alternative pedagogies reflects, in part, its central importance to liberatory and emancipatory discourses.

Mutuality's centrality in progressive, critical, and feminist discourses can be seen in the frequent use of terms such as *empowerment, transaction,* and *reciprocity.* Inherent in these discourses is a reconfiguration of social relations in the classroom that rejects the idea that the teacher's main role is to convey a received body of knowledge to students. Rather, these discourses privilege a transactional approach to knowledge making. Complementing and underwriting this transactional emphasis is a focus on dialogue. Progressive, critical, and feminist discourses position themselves at the intersection of teacher, learner, and knowledge making; in so doing, these approaches implicitly value interaction as a mode of operation in the classroom as they explicitly go after ideological issues (see Lather 121). Mutuality is invoked in that knowledge is not a prepackaged commodity to be delivered by the teacher but is an "outcome" constituted in the classroom through the dialogic interaction among teachers and students alike.

But even though mutuality is central to liberatory and emancipatory discourses, approaches differ regarding what should be the end result of the dialogic interaction among classroom participants and the knowledge constructed through such interaction. Differences concerning the issue of transformation predominate. Dewey, for example, locates the power of knowledge to transform in the ability of individuals to change socially based habits. Thus, Dewey does not see cultural reproduction as either a negative or necessary outcome of the knowledge making or learning. Proponents of Marxist and feminist ideologies, on the other hand, emphasize the inherent and ultimately dangerous connection between education and cultural reproduction (Giroux, "Living Dangerously"). These theorists want education to lead not merely to individual but to cultural transformation. Marxist theorists, including Freire and Giroux, thus insist on actively resisting knowledge as constructed by the dominant culture and emphasize the *transformative* power of knowledge for those who resist. The teacher's role is to raise students' awareness of the social, political, and usually oppressive consequences of education.[3] Feminist theorists also invoke awareness and resistance as educational goals but emphasize that knowledge is transformative in different ways for different people, depending on socially constructed factors such as gender, race, and class. Feminists have been particularly alert to differences in "masculine" and "feminine" ways of knowing and to the different value accorded to these respective ways (e.g., Tuana; Bleich, "Sexism"). Because of their resistance to the reproduction of the dominant culture, both Marxist and feminist philosophies attend to the transformative potential of language and knowledge making in a way that Deweyan approaches (at least as we understand them) do not.

These differences are important for our purposes because issues of cultural reproduction and individual transformation underwrite difficulties that have emerged in trying to implement alternative pedagogies and achieve mutuality in the classroom. Marxist and feminist theorists are historically situated so that they see resistance to cultural reproduction as the appropriate focus to their pedagogies. This focus limits their ability to reach mutuality in the classroom if students are not allowed to decline invitations to critical consciousness. We share many of the same assumptions of liberatory and emancipatory approaches, including an emphasis on transactive knowledge making, on dialogic interaction, and on reciprocity in social relations among classroom participants. However, we believe that those seeking mutuality in the classroom need to find ways to exercise authority so that resistance to the dominant culture isn't the only option open to students. Specifically, we think it crucial that student agency operate in a middle space between students' own experiences and the expectations of the discourse communities in which they will have to achieve voice. For us, mutuality is situated in the postmodern sense: it entails a contingent perspective on knowledge and emphasizes the socially constructed nature of meaning, self, and social roles, including those of teacher and student. In the classroom, mutuality is tied to the realization that (1) knowledge is constituted in the classroom rather than simply brought in as disciplinary constructs and (2) the type of language used to generate this knowledge needs to be transactive in nature. We still see mutuality as potentially transformative, but we don't believe that the nature of that transformation can be designated in advance. Transformation emerges from the ongoing interaction of teachers and students in particular classroom situations.

In this book, we explore how this transformative notion of mutuality can be effected in writing classrooms by three important means: (1) reconstituting classroom speech genres, (2) redesigning the architecture of rhetoric and writing courses, and (3) valuing students' interpretive agency in classroom discourse. Our primary purpose is to define mutuality in alternative pedagogy not as a single approach or a specific set of valued practices but as an on-going process in which teachers and students continually collaborate.

Reconstituting Classroom Speech Genres

A key factor in achieving mutuality in the classroom is moving toward parity in discourse relations without ignoring the real differences in teachers', and students' subjectivities, which entail, in part, the ability to see oneself as a knowledge maker. We believe that for such parity to emerge, the *speech genres* of classroom discourse must be reconstituted. This reconstitution is necessary because traditional patterns of classroom discourse reify transmission models of learning. In so doing, these patterns provide a kind of cultural capital that, unless specifically addressed, undermines the goal of mutuality. To effect mutuality in knowledge making, alternative pedagogies must depart from this teacher-centered default represented in traditional classroom discourse patterns and must attempt, in hooks' terminology, to move students from silence to speech.

In using the concept of speech genres, we acknowledge the influence of language theorist Mikhail Bakhtin. In Bakhtinian terms, classrooms can be seen as "spheres of human activity and communication" in which specific sets of discourse practices or "speech genres" have developed that become generic styles that shape human activity and communication (*Speech Genres* 60). We argue that, because speech genres of traditional classrooms depend on transmission-based rather than transactional models of learning and communication, they are insufficient in effecting the negotiation of meaning and social relations inherent in alternative pedagogies. Also important is that rhetorics, as systems of language, are based on certain perspectives of knowledge making. James Berlin, in fact, concludes that the differences among rhetorics at any given historical moment can be attributed to epistemology: "every rhetorical system is based on epistemological assumptions about the nature of reality, the nature of the knower, and the rules governing the discovery and communication of the known" (*Rhetoric* 3). The type of rhetoric employed in the classroom, then, suggests the type of knowledge making taking place. In addition, because traditional classroom speech genres represent ways of preserving power inequities between teacher and student, they are inappropriate for effecting authority in the classroom that is, to use Mortensen and Kirsch's term, "more democratic" (569). Thus, alternative pedagogies depend not only on an ideological stance that sees teacher and student as co-constructors of knowledge, but also on an understanding that teachers and students, operating on a mutual basis, must work out their multiple subjectivities *within new types of discourse*. This focus on discourse should be particularly attractive to teachers in the rhetoric and composition classroom because it emphasizes the relationship between power and language.

If we can simplify for the moment, in traditional classrooms, language and knowledge making is often reserved for the teacher. Teachers talk and students listen. In other words, knowledge is a matter for teacher transmission, rather than mutual creation involving teacher and students alike. As Courtney Cazden puts it:

> In typical classrooms, the most important asymmetry in the rights and obligations of teacher and students is over control of the right to speak. To describe the difference in the bluntest terms, teachers have the right to speak at any time and to any person; they can fill any silence or interrupt any speaker; they can speak to a student anywhere in

> the room and in any volume or tone of voice. And no one
> has the right to object. But not all teachers assume such
> rights or live by such rules all the time. (54)

In such classrooms, the connection between language and knowledge making thus becomes tied to a transmission model of learning,
often effected through lecture and teacher-dominated discussion,
where teachers convey knowledge to students who receive this
knowledge and, in this way, learn what they need to know.

The focus on knowledge transmission is easy to see in the
speech genre of lecture: teachers cover information, and students
take notes and later regurgitate knowledge in examinations. However, simply eschewing lecture in favor of class discussions in which
students are encouraged to actively participate will not necessarily
lead to mutuality. For example, in the following sequence, J. Sinclair
and R. M. Coulthard (67) demonstrate a pattern of class discussion
in which teachers retain control of what counts as knowledge:

Opening (teacher): Where would you see these signs?
Answering (student): Where the men were digging the road up
    and making an open hole.
Follow-up (teacher): Yes.
Opening (teacher): It's a warning sign, isn't it? It's a warning
    sign, so be careful because further along up the road that
    you're driving on there are workmen digging up the road
    or filling in a hole, doing some work.
Opening (teacher): What's the next one mean? You don't often
    see that one around here. Miri?

The questions here bring together an ideological stance in which
teachers control knowledge with a discourse strategy that attempts
to reduce available subjectivities to match the familiar dichotomy:
teacher as subject and student as object. The questions asked are, by
nature, "inauthentic," to use Martin Nystrand and Adam Gamoran's
term. That is, the teacher does not ask the questions to gain information but to see whether the students know the "right answer."

"Right answers" equal effectively transmitted knowledge. Inauthentic questions can be and, in fact, are asked in traditional classrooms at any given level of achievement. For example, the "opening, response, follow-up" discourse pattern Sinclair and Coulthard observed in secondary classrooms can easily be resituated in a junior-level college class in rhetorical analysis:

Opening (teacher): Where would you see a neo-Aristotelian approach working in analyzing this set of artifacts?
Answering (student): Well, you could see it in the invention.
Follow-up (teacher): Yes.
Opening (teacher): Okay, invention is one of the five departments that Foss [author of the textbook] talks about, right? For invention, you could identify the proofs that involve the various appeals—ethos, pathos, logos. Then you could identify something significant in the author's use of one or more of these appeals.
Opening (teacher): What other departments does Foss discuss? A couple of them don't seem to have immediate application to written texts, do they? Joe?

Within such a setting, disagreement is always due to "faulty observation, faulty language, or both, and never is due to the problematic and contingent nature of truth" (see Berlin, *Rhetoric* 11). This approach, then, focuses instruction on "correct" answers and on mastering received ways of thinking and knowing. Knowledge making for students, and often also for teachers, becomes a matter of assimilating the constructions of others. Transmission rather than transactional models of communicative interaction and learning dominate, and learning becomes an exercise in memorization rather than meaning making.

Not only is teacher control of knowledge possible in such traditional class discussions, but "disciplinary control" over both subject matter and student behavior can also be effected through traditional classroom discourse. In fact, a study by Bellack, Kliebard, Hyman, and Smith provides a de facto definition of teacher authority and control achieved through various types of discourse moves. Their analysis of fifteen tenth- and twelfth-grade classes in metropolitan and suburban New York revealed that discourse used in classrooms allowed the teachers to set nearly all the tasks, initiate the topics for discussion, and strictly control the elaboration of topics through immediate reactions to students' responses. In short, the discourse ensured that the teachers would hold most, if not all, the authority in the classroom.[4]

Subsequent studies by Sinclair and Coulthard and by Hugh Mehan confirm the central role dominant classroom speech genres play in constructing transmission-based rather than transactional learning environments. Sinclair and Coulthard noticed that a "typical exchange" in the classes they examined consisted of teachers Initiating, students Responding, and teachers providing Feedback (IRF), a pattern that effected teacher dominance. Hugh Mehan, who initially criticized Sinclair and Coulthard for focusing almost exclusively on teachers' effort at control and for minimizing the contributions of students, discovered many of the same constituent components: an IRE pattern of teacher student interaction with a teacher's Initiation followed by a student's Reply and a teacher's Evaluation. Although Mehan was able to show students could, at times, gain initiation rights if they managed to seize the floor and then introduce a topic that was seen by the teacher as having sufficient "news" value, his results clearly indicated that IRE typically allowed for strong teacher control (103). In her extensive review of classroom discourse research, Cazden argues that, even as an alternative to lecture, the IRE pattern is so pervasive in American education that it can accurately be called the "default pattern—what happens unless deliberate action is taken to achieve some alternative" (53).

This body of research has led us to conclude that reconstituting the speech genres of classroom discourse is necessary to achieve the goal of mutuality in knowledge making. Certainly, mutuality in knowledge making cannot be achieved within the context of speech genres that privilege teachers' absolute control over what counts for knowledge. To move from what Freire calls the "banking concept of

education" toward a transformed pedagogy where, through dialogue, "the teacher-of-the-students and the students-of-the-teacher
cease to exist and a new term emerges . . . teacher-student with
students-teachers" (*Oppressed*, 61), new patterns of discourse must
be available. A transformed pedagogy cannot exist where the teacher
typically makes two-thirds of the discourse moves. It cannot exist
where the functions open to all classroom participants are assumed
to be limited to *initiation, response,* and *evaluation*. And it cannot
exist where teachers occupy the powerful subject positions as ini-
tiators and evaluators, and students, much less powerful object positions as responders who must match their understandings to the
teacher's expectations or face immediate correction.

Redesigning Course Architecture

For mutuality to emerge, teachers need to do more than reconstitute
the speech genres in their classrooms. They also need to redesign
their course architectures so that teachers and students alike occupy tenable subject positions and share in the meaning making. By
course architecture we mean the management of assignments and
activities that make up the day-to-day procedural functioning of
the class and, in particular, the ways in which classroom assignments and activities encourage (or discourage) interaction among
disciplinary knowledge and students' varied knowledge and experiences. Course architecture that seeks mutuality can be understood
(1) as the teacher's best guess about which assignments and activities will most likely lead to mutuality within a given class and (2)
as the ongoing negotiation of procedures and reconstructions of
knowledge subsequently worked out in specific classroom settings.

   As a concept, course architecture shares with reconstituted
classroom speech genres a concern for subject-subject relations. Reconstituted classroom speech genres invite those assuming subject
positions to operate in the space between disciplinary knowledge
and personal knowledge. Course architecture focuses on how specific assignments and activities can instantiate mutuality among
classroom participants. Course architecture also shares with recon-

stituted classroom speech genres a concern for power. Reconstituted classroom discourse highlights the power of classroom speech genres to give students voice as they find their voices within the voices of the academy. Course architecture involves the extent to which and ways in which teachers will share authority over the basic structure of a course and the assignments and daily activities that comprise it. Sample considerations include

- How much input will students have in deciding the amount of class time spent on such activities as teacher-led discussions, peer review, workshop sessions, and student presentations?
- How much input will students have in the choice of textbooks or other readings for the course?
- How much input will students have in the kinds and topics of writing assignments?
- How much input will students have in the criteria used to assess their performance and determine their grades?

Since there is no magic formula for negotiating power or for effecting subject-subject relations in the design of assignments and activities, teachers might vary widely in their plans for creating mutuality through course architecture.

In general, composition pedagogy has been gradually moving in the direction of course architecture that encourages mutuality, although further development is still needed. With the emergence of the process movement in the 1960s, composition teaching has relied less and less on the teacher-fronted grammar lessons and theme-a-day practices of current traditional rhetoric and has included more teacher-absent activities (e.g., peer review and small group work). Such changes, however, have not in themselves necessarily effected mutuality. The introduction of computer technology into the writing classroom is a case in point. Using computers in the writing classroom was, at least initially, seen to make writing pedagogy more democratic because computers were to empower students and erase gender, race, and class differences. But simply reconfiguring the physical setup of the classroom and introducing electronic forms of class discussion did not necessarily work to effect liberatory and emancipatory goals. Indeed, being riveted to online disciplinary materials posted by the instructor does not free students from lecture; it simply changes how that instruction is delivered. Similarly, participating in networked discussion does not free students from ways of talking that reproduce social relations in the dominant culture; electronic discussion can simply conceal the identity of the speaker, if contributors use pseudonyms, and give everyone the opportunity to use the language of oppression. It should come as no surprise, then, that the early, often simplistic claims for computer pedagogy have since been criticized (see Hawisher and Selfe). The promised utopia of computer pedagogy has yet to emerge (Faigley). The addition of computer technology to the composition classroom—much like the introduction of peer review, small group work, and other pedagogical innovations of the process movement—cannot be seen as a pedagogical revolution in and of itself. Instead, such innovations simply represent tools that expand the repertoire of class assignments and activities available to writing teachers and students and that can be used in course architectures that seek mutuality as a primary goal.

Course architecture that invites mutuality entails implementation of changes that move beyond the use of new techniques to solve old problems. It requires consideration of three issues. First, it entails fundamental change in teacher and student roles. It entails use of an interactive, dialogic model of teaching that curtails teachers' presentational roles while simultaneously enhancing students' leadership in generating knowledge in the classroom. In other words, teachers will negotiate such matters as the nature and number of assignments to be submitted, and students will take more responsibility for wrestling with disciplinary knowledge, for exploring connections between disciplinary knowledge and their own and others' experiences, and for managing the flow of class activities. Such changes will require time and effort to implement as both students and teachers figure out how to function in their new roles.

Second, development of a course architecture that promotes mutuality also entails recognizing that teachers and students will have a range of responses to change that matches the wide range of subjectivities involved. Some teachers, for example, may resist change, simply because they have a repertoire of teaching plans and practices that have served them well in the past. Some students might similarly resist change, wishing that their teacher would simply exercise the kinds of control that the students have come to expect and that have allowed them to achieve high grades in the past. Also, participation in the co-construction of knowledge will not mean the same thing for all teachers and students because of their perceptions of themselves and because of different ways that they are perceived. For example, one 22-year-old, first-time teaching assistant may find sharing authority a natural move because the assistant feels close in age and experience to the students, while another assistant in similar circumstances may find sharing authority dangerous, because students would essentially be invited to question the assistant's disciplinary knowledge.

Finally, in course architectures designed with mutuality in mind, disagreement and resistance are to be expected because such pedagogy encourages the expression of different perspectives and because the nature of authority in such classes has changed. When students are invited to actively express what they think rather than simply accept a dominant view, disagreement, even conflict, is likely. When teachers share authority, the power they exercise is changed. In this regard, Mortensen and Kirsch's distinction between authority as the "power to enforce obedience" and authority as the "power to influence action, opinion, and belief" is helpful (559). In traditional pedagogy, the teacher attempts to maintain the power to enforce obedience by retaining complete control of classroom management. The teacher also assumes control by getting students to accept disciplinary knowledge without question. In alternative pedagogy, a teacher must temper the power to enforce obedience. The teacher may retain the right to intervene only when conflict threatens to undermine the class's sense of community or when students' contributions wander so far afield that connections to disciplinary knowledge become extremely difficult. To an even greater degree, teachers must also share the power to influence action and belief. The teacher's voice becomes just one of many voices articulating how personal experiences and knowledge can usefully interact with representations of disciplinary knowledge. Here, resistance to accepted notions of what constitutes knowledge is a normal part of the process of collaboratively constructing knowledge. Seeing disagreement and resistance as essential ingredients to a class's course architecture may take a little getting used to, even for teachers committed to effecting mutuality in the classroom.

In the writing classroom, acknowledging disagreement and resistance as essential ingredients in course architecture is reflected in current discussions in the discipline regarding conflict and consensus. A number of composition theorists have openly advocated conflict as a basis for investigating and writing about the world. For example, Dennis Lynch, Diana George, and Marilyn Cooper value conflict as a way of making the writing classroom "a place to engage in serious intellectual inquiry and debate about the questions that trouble our everyday lives" (84). In so doing, they seek a way of reconceiving argument that includes "both confrontational and cooperative perspectives" (63). Others have explored the basic assumption that classrooms should be "relatively safe and cooperative places" (see Fishman and McCarthy 342). Susan Jarratt, for example, objects to attempts to sidestep conflict in the classroom; she argues such attempts to avoid conflict often mean that sexist and racist student language goes unchallenged "in classes which establish supportive and accepting climates" (105–6). Jarratt, like hooks, sees classroom conflict as essential to social change (see hooks, "Teaching" 42). Both value dissensus and see consensus as inherently promoting the status quo. Other critics point out that attempts to avoid conflict are often dismissive of students' points of view, if these viewpoints depart from those acceptable in the dominant culture. Richard Miller notes that "dominant assumptions about students and student writing allow unsolicited oppositional discourse to pass through the classroom unread and unaffected" (391). Miller argues that traditional teachers often grade student writing by registering how well it meets assignment criteria and how well it displays the rhetorical and grammatical strategies appropriate to the expected final product. While such an approach allows both teacher and student to remain in the "contact zone" of the classroom,[5] it also sidesteps the problem of responding to the "parodic, critical, oppositional, dismissive, resistant, transgressive, and regressive writing" that gets produced there (394). In contrast, the alternative classroom invites disagreement and resistance. Furthermore, the problem of responding to oppositional discourses becomes not only the *teacher's* problem when evaluating papers or leading discussions, but also *each participant's* problem when responding to others in the class. And while some students may become "guarded" or polite in voicing their opinions once they realize that they are speaking about issues that threaten group cooperation or damage ongoing relationships (see Fishman and McCarthy 363), we believe that inviting disagreement and resistance, while crucial, is inherently risky pedagogical practice.

Valuing Interpretive Agency

Achieving mutuality requires teachers and students alike to recognize and value the role interpretive agency—their own and that of others—plays in knowledge making in the classroom. At this point it might be useful to distinguish *agency* from *interpretive agency.* Agency is the ability to influence class tasks and topics as well as the ability to influence the choices that individual writers (including oneself) make. Interpretive agency involves bringing one's prior experience to bear in the construction of knowledge. An individual's interpretive agency depends on his or her unique perspective, which, in turn, is based on the set of life experiences that each person brings to classroom discourse or other communicative events. Although the concepts of agency and interpretive agency are clearly related in practice, the distinction is important in sorting out how differences in individuals' unique subjectivities affect the kinds of agency that can take place in school settings. Often American education attempts to codify a student's past experience and, in so doing, to co-opt individual experiences in disciplinary frameworks or to reduce students' individualities to a common set of traits, skills, or pieces of knowledge that all students are expected to master. From such a perspective, students' mastery of a carefully defined curriculum is the test of learning. In fact, the idea that there are definite skills to be mastered is implicit in college writing programs. The academy instituted first-year composition in the first place out of a belief that incoming students lack basic skills. In other words, the course's founding assumption discourages its teachers from recognizing what students can contribute to it.[6] In contrast, alternative pedagogies assume learning begins at the intersection of students' knowledge and experiences and the teachers' representations of disciplinary knowledge. Students' interpretive agency is valued because it is one of the primary bases on which knowledge is constructed (or reconstructed). There is not necessarily a single set of facts to be learned or a single posture, such as resistance, to be assumed. Given the diverse assumptions underpinning writing programs in the academy and alternative pedagogies in the individual classroom, the presence of alternative approaches in writing classes is problematic, especially in those institutional settings where writing instructors do not have the freedom to design their own syllabi or to determine course content. At the same time, alternative approaches have the power to suggest classroom practices that can effect liberatory and emancipatory goals, even in restrictive environments.

Overall, we see three important implications of valuing students' interpretive agency as the starting point for learning. First, valuing interpretive agency changes the nature of teacher authority in the classroom. In traditional classrooms, teachers serve as the source of disciplinary knowledge and as the determiners of the extent to which students have achieved mastery of that knowledge.[7] This view of learning, based on a transmission model, awards teachers the status as subject-knowers, with students the objects of knowledge that is made by others. Valuing students' interpretive agency shifts the focus of instruction. Instead of concentrating on students' mastery of discrete units of received knowledge, instruction constitutes and reflects the knowledge being made at the intersection of students' varied experiences and disciplinary knowledge.

For mutuality to develop at these intersections, disciplinary knowledge must thus be regarded as a work in progress. In addition, the subject-object distinction between teachers and students must break down to the extent that all classroom participants have the opportunity to assume subject status, even though these subjectivities will differ. For example, a writing teacher might assume subject status by selecting textbooks and course readings, by asking students to explore certain diversity issues, and by assigning final grades. Students in this setting might, as subjects, generate their own topics, privilege certain rhetorical strategies and genres, and participate in peer review and personal performance appraisals based on student-designated evaluation criteria. Subject status is thus accorded to teacher and students alike, even though power relations may remain asymmetrical.

Valuing student input does not necessarily threaten a teacher's status, because a teacher's authority is vested not in an obligation to transmit culturally received knowledge to students, but in the teacher's greater experience in understanding and constituting such knowledge. That teachers by definition have this experience remains one of the critical components in teachers' subjectivities. When disciplinary knowledge, as well as other knowledge, is seen as continuously under construction, inviting students to take a role in that construction does not represent a terrible threat. Indeed, Dewey was not afraid to insist that education, while beginning with students' experiences, have as its goal disciplinary knowledge, which he saw as a continuous weaving together of past and present (see *Later* 13: 53; Russell 186). Moreover, as indicated previously, teachers and students sharing authority does not necessarily mean power parity. Feminist theorist Madeleine Grumet, in fact, argues that the teacher's privilege is not only inherent but also necessary in the classroom and that it is this very asymmetry that actually allows the dialogue between teacher and student to "enlarge our collective consciousness" (97). Teachers in writing classrooms exercise their privilege by creating occasions for writing and by establishing strategies and discussing situated standards for textual production and review. The disciplinary advantage they enjoy, however, entails the interaction that occurs when classroom participants work together to effect progress in students' evolving work and when teachers and students alike assist in making textual improvements.

Secondly, valuing students' interpretive agency makes untenable romantic notions of agency in which student empowerment is equated with individually achieved self-fulfillment. Valuing interpretive agency in the classroom means that individual authority is not autonomous but is informed by participants' divergent perspectives. As participants in knowledge making, students must engage perspectives that are different from their own, whether those perspectives are expressed by a teacher or by a peer. Given this context, a romantic sense of agency is problematic in that it downplays the intimate role others play in personal achievements, the role interaction plays in learning, and, indeed, the role society plays in the very construction of self. In the history of education, it is this very sense of independent agency that Dewey attacked. In composition studies, it is a romantic sense of agency that, to some degree, is implicated in the debate between David Bartholomae and Peter Elbow. Their argument centers on whether we can write and run writing classrooms "without teachers." Invoking a romantic sense of agency, Elbow believes that student writers benefit from seeing "their papers as monologues or soliloquies" (79) when composing. In contrast, Bartholomae invokes a social sense of self, emphasizing that neither teachers nor students can escape the social power of institutions in their classes and their writing ("Writing"). In this book, we align ourselves with the social perspective. We see both teachers and students as constructed subjects or agents in the classroom. We thus resist the romantic version of those approaches in progressive education—variously termed student-centered or child-centered pedagogy—which see education's goal as that of liberating the individual student from the teacher's control, from the constraints of society, or even from a sense of responsibility to one's peers. Instead, like Dewey and Vygotsky, we see self-realization as achieved through society, "though it may involve resisting one set of social practices (habits, ideologies) in favor of another, more useful set" (see Russell 184–85). We believe that achieving this self-realization through society means that, on an ongoing basis, teachers and students are mutually working out what counts for knowledge in the classroom. In addition, we acknowledge that seeing the nature of knowledge and knowing as fluid and dynamic here reflects a postmodern emphasis on situatedness, on the constructive nature of language, and on the constructed nature of society and self.

Achieving such self-realization has often been associated in the writing classroom with the concept of voice. As a metaphor, voice has been used in rhetoric and composition literature to talk about the writer composing text, the writer revealing cultural knowledge in his or her composing choices, and the writer discovering "an authentic self and then deploying it in the text" (Yancey vii). Donald Graves, Donald Murray, and Peter Elbow have discussed voice as a force within the individual writer that, when tapped, drives the writing process. Others, such as William Coles and Jane Tompkins, have discussed voice in social or collectivist terms as a "fluid composite of cultural voices and individual selves within the writer" (Yancey xi). Such differences point to a difficulty inherent in the concept of voice when applied to individual students, namely that voicing necessarily involves words, and every word, to use Bakhtin's language, "gives off the scent of a profession, a genre, a current, a party, a particular work, a particular man, a generation, an era, a day, and an hour. Every word smells of the context and contexts in which it has lived its intense social life" (Todorov 56).[8] When writers use language, they necessarily engage or respond to past and present discourses. In other words, language embodies both individual and community voices, and individual voices contain community voices, and the notion that an autonomous, Cartesian self can provide the basis for a purely unique individual voice becomes untenable. Yet—despite Michel Foucault's dramatic claim—the author lives. Even though each writer is in a sense written by cultural forms, writers still write. Thus, for students in writing classes, attaining voice means more than coming to understand how they are socially and culturally constructed and how their unique subjectivities affect their constructions of others. It also means more than simply learning "basic skills" of grammar and punctuation or features of various genres. Voices emerge in mutuality—in pedagogical practices that bring students' current understandings together with culturally valued representations of knowledge in classroom talk and in writing assignments and activities. The voices that develop under these conditions are continually recreated and exist between the extremes of the student as an autonomous self and the student as the passive recipient of knowledge.

A third implication of valuing students' interpretive agency is that the ends of education cannot be predetermined in any absolute sense. We have already implied that actively engaging students as interpretive agents precludes transmission models of learning in which predefined pieces of knowledge are to be presented and mastered. However, valuing student agency also impinges on the goals of Marxist and feminist pedagogies where cultural critique is the expected result of instruction. Overall, we see the resistance that is the goal of critical and feminist pedagogies as too often representing a binary choice: teachers must demonstrate resistance by reacting against the dominant culture or they can be judged as acting outside liberatory and emancipatory discourses. Students can demonstrate resistance by following the teacher's lead in reacting against the dominant culture or risk being labeled as reactionary. In alternative approaches, critique cannot be named the primary or sole outcome of education, because privileging resistance can in itself become an expression of a teacher's absolute authority if it, too, is not up for negotiation. The irony here is that the attenuation of teacher authority necessary for valuing students' interpretive agency may require, at times, that teachers support students' attempts to represent positions that run contrary to a teacher's liberatory goals.

Our position on resistance here might be viewed by some as further co-opting the critical pedagogy movement by allowing teachers and students alike to feel okay about learning disciplinary knowledge without the required political critique essential to Marxist and feminist approaches. Whereas Marxists seek to reconfigure oppressive socioeconomic structures and feminists similarly look to reconstruct power relations in society (but with the specific goal of incorporating women's perspectives and improving women's status), we seek neither a predesignated end for the social critique that manifests itself in various ways in our pedagogical approach nor a single-faceted resistance. Resistance to cultural reproduction is only one of a number of valid options open to our students. For example, after students have developed the habit of occupying subject positions in the classroom, they well might resist a teacher's assignments or evaluation criteria based on their relevance to the students' construction of knowledge. Such resistance shows students bringing their own agenda to bear on classroom business. In valuing that agenda, we open the door for a range of ideologically based outcomes to emerge in the alternative classroom.

Valuing interpretive agency in the classroom leads to a view of resistance that is based on relevance. It is a relevance located in classroom assignments and activities, and situated at the intersection of disciplinary knowledge and the students' knowledge and experience. This relevance, tied as it is to the multiple subjectivities and difference embodied in students' knowledge and experience, will be diversely defined and understood. In short, the choices for resistance will be many and part of the ongoing act of meaning making in the classroom. Even so, valuing students' interpretive agency does not mean that anything goes. Teachers have both the right and the responsibility to demonstrate to a class that participants' contributions to classroom discourse must respect the values and perspectives of others (although it is also true that teachers can undermine student agency by intervening too frequently and too directly in class discussions). In addition, teachers generally have considerable leeway in how they choose to represent disciplinary knowledge. For example, in composition instruction, many writing teachers—influenced by feminist theory—have recognized the "phallocentric" nature of many disciplinary rhetorics (Hollis) and have established a link between the personal essay and feminine forms of knowledge and expression that weave together rational and emotive thought (Zawacki). Some have called for the adoption of writing that allows for multiple truths—multidimensional reality— rather than a single thesis (Bridwell-Bowles) and for negotiation and mediation rather than monologic claim making (Lamb). Similarly, others involved in composition pedagogy have followed the lead of critical theorists and considered the implications of resistance to culturally received interpretations of academic discourse. Rhetoric and composition classrooms are a particularly rich site for studying the struggle to be alternative for several reasons. For one thing, attempts at liberatory and emancipatory pedagogies in the writing classroom are characteristically based on the realization that the signifying practices in the classroom help define who we are, what is good, and what is possible (see Berlin, "Poststructuralism" 23). Thus, because rhetoric is both the subject and the vehicle of instruction in these classrooms, language as a component of knowledge making can hardly be ignored. Writing teachers have seen in the Marxist drive for resistance the need to be aware of the cultural reproduction implicit in teaching received genres in academic and professional discourse and the need to rewrite how authority is situated in the composition classroom. Teachers using alternative approaches can similarly express agendas of their own.

In sum, we see valuing students' interpretive agency as a definitive step in achieving mutuality. From this perspective, strategies such as abandoning lecture in favor of class discussions, teacher-student conferences, peer group work, tutoring sessions, and other methodologies have the potential to focus classroom discourse on the intersections between disciplinary knowledge and students' unique subjectivities as the starting point for learning. But these strategies do not, in themselves, guarantee the emergence of mutuality. In this regard, Bartholomae laments the history of surface rather than substantive change in the composition classroom. He argues that it is not enough to "rearrange the furniture" or even "rearrange the turns taken by speakers" in classroom discourse if these actions "have no immediate bearing on the affiliations of power brought into play in writing" ("Writing" 66). As Bartholomae's critique implies, valuing students' interpretive agencies while still accounting for the real constraints of culture on individuals' agency is a difficult business. Writing pedagogies that would achieve mutuality cannot feature disciplinary representations of knowledge to the point that students' interpretive agency atrophies. Nor can these pedagogies glorify students' agency to the point that disciplinary representations of knowledge become irrelevant.

Acknowledging Potential and Risk

While specific benefits and risks of alternative pedagogies are discussed in subsequent chapters, we can initially observe here that potential benefits include the engaging of students as interpretive agents and knowledge makers and the enfranchising of members of marginalized groups. Both of these benefits involve the issue of transformation by introducing a new role for students in classroom communities as well as by empowering individuals traditionally occupying object positions in society. Indeed, a primary benefit of achieving mutuality involves creating opportunities to value alternative ways of knowing. As Mary Field Belenky, Blythe McVicker Clinchy, Nancy Rule Goldberger, and Jill Mattuck Tarule have argued, students bring very different images of themselves as knowers, images developed in the discourse of previous school and family interactions. Applied to college writing courses, their work suggests that classroom discourse must be dialogic[9] if students are to be engaged in knowledge making that fosters the development of self through integration with others. In other words, mutuality in knowledge making must not only recognize that differences in ways of knowing exist but must also value those differences as part of the process of reconstituting knowledge in classroom discourse. Such a view of learning attempts to enfranchise all students while still allowing teachers to represent the value and costs of participating in the discourse practices expected in higher education.

While we acknowledge the potential of alternative pedagogies, we must also acknowledge the risks of departing from a teacher-centered default. The move to an interactive pedagogy does not ensure that certain subject positions when assumed by students are safe. For example, John Trimbur criticizes critical pedagogies for ignoring the safety issue in idealizing resistance. Trimbur believes that liberatory pedagogies have ignored the social costs of such resistance. It is one thing for students to "have a right to their own language" and quite another for students to use idiosyncratic grammar on letters of job application. Another set of risks involves the risk entailed when students assume subject positions. For example, students, once given a voice or authority, might employ strategies that could be considered oppressive (see Freire, *Oppressed*). When students assume subject positions, there is no guarantee that they will allow each other to speak freely, be open to each other's arguments, trust each other's interpretations, and value each other's contributions.

Teachers using alternative approaches also place themselves at risk in terms of how they are evaluated. Indeed, those who teach in American primary and secondary schools, as well as those who train such teachers, must be aware that the dominant view of education in our country is implicitly hostile to teachers' attempts to share authority with students over what counts as knowledge. For example, when educational innovations are reported on the nightly news or in the popular press, improvements in students' standardized test scores are often given as evidence of the innovation's effectiveness—a practice supported by a multimillion-dollar educational testing industry. These standardized tests in turn reinforce the close connection between a transmission model of knowledge making and traditional speech genres in American education by testing procedures that value the reproduction of culturally determined knowledge over creative or critical thinking. Although we believe that teachers at all levels of American education should engage their students as co-constructors of knowledge, we also recognize that doing so may be more difficult for those whose teaching is assessed in terms of students' standardized test scores than for those whose teaching is assessed differently. In higher education, using alternative pedagogies might be difficult for teachers of first-year composition, because first-year writing teachers are frequently graduate students and part-timers. The risks of using alternative approaches are significant for members of the academic underclass of limited-term appointees—what Susan Miller terms the "rotating bottom" of composition faculty (146). As such, often they must teach a preestablished syllabus, and the academy marginalizes them in sundry other ways. Their willingness to practice mutuality in their classrooms might easily be affected by the *lack* of mutuality they experience in their everyday working conditions. Certainly, those of us who teach writing and rhetoric courses as tenure-line faculty (or who prepare graduate students to do so) often have more freedom to design the kinds of courses that we see fit without the immediate pressure of any formal outcomes assessment.

Yet college teaching is not necessarily a wonderland for alternative pedagogy for even tenure-line instructors. Administrators can still use teacher evaluation to discourage or encourage alternative pedagogical practice. Indeed, one of the reasons that we began this project was observed inequities in the evaluation of tenure-line faculty who used alternative pedagogy. In serving on our department's tenure and promotion committee, Helen noted that if a faculty member simply handed in syllabi that listed readings and assignments for courses and included a sample set of lecture notes, then the committee found it quite easy to approve the teaching materials. Teachers did not have to justify lecture as a technique, either to the committee or, in a majority of the cases, to the students. Students raved about instructors who "gave good notes," who "answered all their questions," and who, as a bonus, were entertaining besides (cf. Tompkins' performance model). However, those engaged in alternative teaching generated considerable controversy and, even, hostility. Helen's experience embodies the risks alternative teachers face, especially when being evaluated under old assumptions about what makes for good teaching and what constitutes student learning.

Such risks make the task of establishing mutuality in the classroom infinitely more complex, especially when we consider the potential costs of mutuality for teachers and students of marginalized groups. How mutuality creates risk can be understood by looking at David Bleich's discussion of reciprocity. Bleich adamantly insists that "teachers and students should be considered members of the *same class*" (*Double* 253). For Bleich, the reciprocity that emerges from this relationship between teacher and student entails the "mutual assimilation of memory and experience" where classrooms are "best understood through the double perspectives of private and public, oral and written viewpoints" (*Double* 90, 192). Within this context, collaborative interaction and interpretation work to produce a "stereoscopic view" that introduces a third space where cultural production (rather than reproduction) occurs. If Bleich is right—and we suspect that he is—creating a new set of instructional possibilities depends on bringing together students' and teachers' personal histories with the public discourse of instruction. As a consequence, the development of alternative patterns of classroom discourse is likely to be at once more problematic and more critical for women or other groups of students whose backgrounds have not prepared them to find voices within traditional classroom discourse. Despite the risks inherent to engaging a range of subjectivities through classroom talk, we see still such engagement as essential to effecting mutuality in classroom knowledge making. To be sure, it is an engagement that must be entered carefully; our aim is to help our readers make considered choices in accepting the challenge that mutuality represents.

Investigating Mutuality in Our Classrooms

In the chapters that follow, we explore mutuality in alternative pedagogies by focusing on the issues of speech genres, course architecture, and interpretive agency. Our purpose is to investigate how these concepts can be implemented, and our exploration is based on our study of two classrooms where we were consciously attempting to employ alternative pedagogies. Participants included us as teachers and our students in two rhetoric classes at Iowa State University. We chose to focus this investigation on two of our own courses both because we wanted to understand our own teaching practices better and because we felt that we needed to subject our own practice to critique before we could suggest the same to others.

David's class was an entry-level first-year college writing course. This class had twenty-seven participants—David and twenty-six first-year students. Fifteen of the participants (including David) were of European-American descent; five were African American; four were Asian and nonnative speakers of English, and three were Puerto Rican (bilingual in English and Spanish). Helen's class was a graduate course in communication theory. The class had ten participants—Helen and nine graduate students. All the participants were of European-American descent; one was male, and nine female. We chose these courses partly for the contrast between the participants and partly because they were courses we were both very comfortable teaching.

We observed and tape-recorded five meetings of each other's class during a semester and conducted interviews after each observed class meeting with each other and with two students from each class whom we had selected as case study participants. These participants, Sam and Penny from Helen's class and Ann and Laura from David's, were selected according to a survey that determined their contrasting initial preferences for teacher control and their comfort with active participation in classroom discourse. With the exception of the first-day observations, we did not know in advance when our classes would be observed. Before the semester began, however, we discussed our syllabi and course schedules in some detail to identify the different kinds of classroom activities (e.g., lecture, class discussion of readings, peer review, student presentations) that were likely to occur on specific days. Because we wanted to represent the range of different kinds of classroom discourse events that would occur in our classes, we checked with each other about every two weeks to see whether the class schedule had changed. We focused on teacher-present classroom discourse because we believe that to effect mutuality, classroom speech genres must first and foremost be reconstituted in whole class settings. The type of discourse used in such settings where both teacher and students are present establishes the tone for language use in other classroom venues. As researchers, we tried to affect the sessions we observed as little as possible. Mostly we sat quietly taking notes and audio-taped each observed class meeting using a small portable tape recorder for later transcription. The audio recordings of the ten class meetings that we observed were transcribed by a professional typist.

We checked each transcript against the original audio recording for accuracy.

We are very much aware that our exploration is limited to two unique contexts. Therefore, we do not intend in this book to provide a single definition of mutuality here or to hold up the classrooms we studied as exemplary models of alternative pedagogy in action. Rather, the discussion of our attempts to engage our students in alternative pedagogy explores how mutuality emerged or failed to emerge in our classrooms. In chapter 2, we examine the problem of reenvisioning discourse rights in the classroom by exploring the nature of the speech genres used in classrooms where teachers are attempting to implement classroom talk that departs from a teacher-centered default. Our focus on classroom speech genres moves us away from methodologies that simply reconfigure furniture arrangements or even classroom participant arrangements to effect liberatory and emancipatory goals. At the same time, it points us to an area of concern—language—that has been at once recognized as crucial to knowledge making and ignored as essential to effecting change in ways of making knowledge in the classroom. That is, not only is there an intimate connection between language and knowledge making, but there is also an intimate connection between the types of language we employ in the classroom and the types of learning that takes place.

In chapter 3, we explore how course architecture can encourage mutuality in the writing classroom. Our discussion here emphasizes the importance of defining mutuality in terms of subject relations that allow for a range of subject positions to be assumed by classroom participants in their interactions. The analysis includes specific examples of writing assignments and activities for both graduate rhetoric and first-year composition courses and students' individual reactions to several of those assignments. Chapter 4 focuses on the part interpretive agency plays in an evolving sense of teacher and student roles in the alternative classroom. Our discussion of interpretive agency provides a picture of student agency that is socially situated rather than individually based and is, indeed, constructed in the classroom. This discussion acknowledges that interpretation happens, even in highly structured classroom environments that feature the teacher wielding disciplinary authority to effect cultural reproduction. Thus, it is the valuing of interpretive agency that helps it contribute to mutuality in knowledge making. Specifically, this chapter explores a particularly inflammatory incident in one of David's class sessions and discusses how four students' as well as David's gender, race, and social class affected the interpretations of David's decision to tell a story about reverse discrimination. Finally, in chapter 5, we situate our vision of mutuality in the discipline. In so doing, we suggest that mutuality is a process for our field, in which teaching as a practice is a leading moment in the formation of what the discipline will become.[10]

2 / Toward Alternative Speech Genres for Classroom Discourse

> The wealth and diversity of speech genres are boundless because the various possibilities of human activity are inexhaustible, and because each sphere of activity contains an entire repertoire of speech genres that differentiate and grow as the particular sphere develops and becomes more complex.
>
> —Mikhail Bakhtin,
> "The Problem of Speech Genres"

> [T]o grant equal classroom time to female students, to democratize the classroom speech situation, and to encourage marginal groups to make public what is personal and private does not alter theoretically or practically those gendered structural divisions upon which liberal capitalism and its knowledge industries are based.
>
> —Carmen Luke,
> "Feminist Politics in Radical Pedagogy"

Developing new speech genres for classroom discourse is essential for effecting alternative pedagogies. Fortunately, as Bakhtin argues in his epigraph, the speech genres in any given sphere are not fixed. Thus, if teachers and students are willing to engage in a wider range of subjectivities than those in traditional classroom discourse, they can work out new ways of interaction and building knowledge despite the larger cultural values that might mitigate against such change. However, as Luke's epigraph suggests, those who do attempt to engage a wider range of subjectivities in the classroom must realize that the intent to be inclusive does not automatically erase social and cultural power differences. Because such differences are embodied in gender, race, class, sexual orientation, as well as other factors, developing new classroom speech genres must entail more than surface-level change. For example, the concept of students having voice must move beyond the basic sense of being able to express opinions and feelings in the classroom. Although a person's having the opportunity to speak is basic to having the authority to make one's past experience and current vision known to others (see Schniederwind), it is not a guarantee that what that person says will be valued as knowledge. Received knowledge, for instance, often excludes women's experiences (Sarachild). Where received or disciplinary knowledge is given priority, it might not matter how much "voice" a woman had, since her ability to negotiate and translate her personal experiences and relationships would ultimately count for very little in a patriarchal scheme of things (see Brady).

In addition, simply providing students with the opportunity to talk with each other without the teacher being present, as in peer groups, does not ensure genuine dialogue among the participants. As Elizabeth Ellsworth notes, the Marxist formula for dialogue, which

> requires and assumes a classroom of participants unified on the side of the subordinated against the subordinators, sharing and trusting in an "us-ness" against "them-ness," does not confront dynamics of subordination present among classroom participants, and within classroom participants, in the form of multiple and contradictory subject positions. (106)

This formula, in other words, does not entertain the notion that a white, middle-class male student might bring to a group situation the personal privilege he enjoys in the society at large. As a group member, he does not have to view himself as "the other," especially if faced with women and minorities as peers. The discourse rights he enjoys as a white male could allow him to retain his own position of privilege and to reproduce the social relations of the culture at large within his peer group.

One of the reasons why moving to different classroom discourse practices is risky, in fact, is that changes in interactional patterns in classrooms do not automatically alter the power structures of society as a whole that are brought into the classroom. The classroom discourse excerpt that will be examined in chapter 4, for example, illustrates that a teacher's invitations to students to express their interpretive agency do not erase differences of gender, race, and class that affect the way the participants respond to statements made in class. Nor do such invitations automatically grant equal authority to participants' contributions. But engaging in alternative speech genres involves risks for all participants, even for those who have been privileged either because of their gender, race, or sociocultural status or because they have developed classroom discourse competencies that have afforded them voice in traditional pedagogy. While changing such traditional patterns carries the potential of enfranchising traditionally marginalized groups and of inviting all students to express their interpretive agency in knowledge making, it also triggers the loss of a set of discourse practices and classroom roles developed over time in thousands of American classrooms. With this loss, teachers and students alike must remake themselves in terms of new competencies.

What, exactly, might these new competencies entail? There can be no single answer to this question. Pedagogy that engages students as mutual knowledge makers defies a simple set of descriptive markers because it begins at the site of the interactions of the unique interpretive agencies of its participants. Such pedagogy is likely to spawn a wide range of classroom discourse practices, which might even include limited roles for lecture and IRE discussions. The exact form that alternative pedagogy takes in any given situation will be influenced by factors including class size; the mix of gender, race, ethnicity, and sexual orientation in the class; curricular constraints; institutional context; teachers' perceptions of their own and students' roles as knowledge makers; and students' age, experience, expectations, and perceptions of themselves as knowledge makers. Yet if the term *alternative pedagogy* is to have any meaning, we must find ways to describe how it is different from traditional pedagogy in the speech genres that comprise it.

Exploring New Speech Genres for Alternative Pedagogy

We see three basic ways of assessing the extent to which pedagogy in a given class has moved away from traditional interaction and toward speech genres in which students and teachers share authority over knowledge. The first and most general indication of such a move is the extent to which students and teachers share the floor. Mutuality seems unlikely if students do not have more than their traditional one-third of conversation turns in a classroom discussion and do not get to speak in ways other than direct responses to teachers' inquiries. Secondly, the extent to which a given pedagogy is alternative can be seen in how students and teachers share control of basic classroom tasks and the initiation and elaboration of topics. Again, if teachers simply allowed students to talk more but not to have input into what gets talked about, then there may be little substantive difference between the patterns of interaction that emerge and the traditional speech genres of lecture and IRE discussion. Finally, there must be indications of reciprocity in evaluation. If students' contributions remain the focus of the majority of the evaluative discourse moves, then students will quickly learn that the game has not really changed that much.

In practice, it is nearly impossible for a teacher to assess the extent to which his or her attempts at change are successful in altering patterns of interaction because the engaging and ongoing nature of teaching leaves little time for on-the-spot reflection. We found that the easiest way to use these three issues to examine our own teaching was to observe each other's classes. Thus, one purpose for the explorations that we subsequently report is to provide a model for other teachers to engage in similar explorations of what new classroom discourse speech genres might "look" like. Others' explorations need not involve the elaborate audiotaping, transcribing, and coding that we did. Observations and running tallies of who gets to talk, when cross-talk breaks out, who initiates tasks and topics, and how evaluation is handled would likely suffice.

A second purpose for these analyses is to provide starting points for other teachers in considering the kinds of changes that might be necessary for new classroom discourse speech genres to emerge. Such changes need not reproduce exactly the ones we describe. As we noted in chapter 1, our descriptions are inextricably bound to the two settings that we examined. Thus, there is neither a single definitive description of new speech genres for alternative pedagogy nor one model for others to follow. Rather, the commonalities that we draw from these two attempts to engage students as knowledge makers make inroads into the largely uncharted territory that lies between teacher dominance and teacher absence in classroom discourse.

Our classes make for an interesting comparison because of the differences between them. Helen's graduate communication theory class was small (ten participants), and David's first-year composition course was large (twenty-seven participants). Helen's class was homogenous in terms of race and nearly in terms of gender (only one participant was male); David's class had a mix of races (although the majority still appeared to be white) and was evenly balanced in terms of gender. At the time of our examinations, Helen had been teaching for seventeen years in various contexts and had developed a case analysis methodology that allowed her to turn over considerable control of the class to her students. For about the first two-thirds of this graduate course, Helen used a case analysis methodology in which her students read brief case narratives and sets of scholarly articles, wrote their own analyses of the cases, and then met with her for discussions. The remaining third of the class was spent in group projects. For about two weeks, the class did not formally meet; rather the teams worked on their projects independently or met with Helen for team conferences. The last two weeks of the course were spent on the team's presentations to the class.

In contrast, David had been teaching at ISU for only two

semesters (he had been a teaching assistant during his Ph.D. program) and his class was more traditional in the sense that David planned the basic structure of each class session. As tenure-track faculty, David could take just about any approach to the course that he wanted; he chose a rather traditional problem-solving approach that fit well with the writing program's goal of preparing students for academic writing. He used a basic process-centered approach in his course, focusing on planning, drafting, and revising; his text was Linda Flower's *Problem Solving Strategies for Writing*. His three major writing assignments—a problem analysis, a thesis-support paper, and a proposal—were all expository in nature. The class featured lots of peer group work, teacher-student conferences, and whole class discussions in which David tried to get students to take the lead in discussions.

The question of how "radical" our courses were is an interesting one. For example, the case narratives and course readings in Helen's graduate class included issues of gender, race, and class, but Helen's teaching method left it to the students to choose what issues they wished to focus on. Thus, the extent to which Helen's course addressed the subject matter often associated with feminist, Marxist, and liberatory pedagogy depended to a large extent on the interests of her students. Because Helen had used this approach many times, she knew she could trust her students to raise interesting issues working within the structure that she set up. David's first-year writing class is probably best described as "traditional" in terms of its content. Nearly all of the students' writing was expository; there was no multicultural reader to raise issues of gender, race, and class, and David did not negotiate the nature of assignments or course readings.

In our eyes, then, these courses had the potential to be alternative, not because we insisted that our students consider Marxist or feminist content but because we used our teacherly authority to set up class situations that invited students to actively construct knowledge with us. Accordingly, we consciously eschewed the traditional classroom discourse genres of lecture and IRE discussion and set up situations that required our students to take active roles in knowledge making. For example, Helen's case analysis method forced her students to apply what they gleaned from reading articles to the case narratives that she provided. In the case analyses that the students wrote *before* class discussion of a case began, they were required to identify primary and secondary issues from the readings and the case narratives that they were then prepared to raise in class discussion.

David used peer review, class discussion, and group work activities to get his students to engage in the construction of knowledge. For example, on each of nine days scattered throughout the course, David assigned three students to do minipresentations of their progress on the current writing assignment. His goal was to get the students to explore a wide range of possibilities for meeting the requirements of the genre of the current assignment. Sometimes these sessions came early in an assignment during activities devoted to invention. Other times they came later in the writing process when students could talk about particular problems that they had encountered in their drafts. To encourage student discussion, David often invoked his "two-response rule": that he could not respond substantively (that is, do more than allot turns or ask clarifying questions) until at least two students had made substantive comments.

In both courses, activities such as peer review or team projects enabled us as teachers simply to step out of the picture and let our students work. Rather than focusing on these activities though, we look in our analyses at whole-class, teacher-present discourse. We believe that unless teachers set a tone in whole-class discussions that invites students to actively express their interpretive agency, then there is little hope of creating new speech genres for classroom discourse that will allow true mutuality to emerge. Specifically, we examine the following three questions as practical means for exploring how the discourse in these two very different classes departed from the traditional speech genres of lecture and IRE discussion:

- To what extent did students and teachers share the floor?
- To what extent did students and teachers introduce basic classroom tasks and initiate or elaborate topics?
- To what extent was there reciprocity in evaluation?

Sharing the Floor

The simplest indication of a departure from traditional classroom speech genres and a move toward mutuality is reflected in the extent to which teachers share the floor with students. In a class dominated by lecture and IRE-style discussion, teachers have two-thirds of the conversation turns or more. Thus, as a rule of thumb, students must take more than one-third of the conversation turns if something other than traditional pedagogy is likely to occur (Cazden).

To assess the extent to which we shared the floor with our students, we did three things. First, we simply tallied the number of conversation turns taken by teachers and students as recorded in the transcripts. We defined a conversation turn as the words or other verbal communication (including silences) used by a person to hold the floor or to bid for the floor. Second, we noted the number of long conversation turns (more than one minute) taken by students and teachers, and third, we counted the number of turns in which students spoke directly to each other in cross-talk (talk without the intervention of a teacher).[1] Previous classroom discourse research suggests that the number and length of conversation turns taken by any one participant indicate the degree and extent of the speaker's authority (Bellack, Kliebard, Hyman, and Smith). Also, the emergence and extent of cross-talk serves as an additional signal of students sharing control of the floor, since students in American primary and secondary schools rarely get the opportunity to engage in cross-talk and seldom share the authority to speak without a teacher's mediation. (Cazden; Lemke).

One of the most interesting things that we discovered when we compared results across the five sessions of each class we examined was that we both dominated the first meetings of our courses. Both of us used long lecture turns in which we spoke from our syllabi, explaining the structure of our courses; there was very little cross-talk among the students in either course on the first day. Ironically, one purpose of these initial sessions was to announce our intentions not to conduct the courses in this traditional manner. As David put it in one of his minilecture turns:

> Very few days in class will I be standing up here and lecturing at you the whole time, telling you how to be a good writer, because nobody learns how to be a good writer by having somebody else tell them how to be a writer. Some days I will stand up here and explain things, but it is much more likely what we'll be doing is pulling the chairs around into a circle, doing exercises where I'm not telling you what the answer is because there is no single answer to the problem or to the question that we're doing.

The patterns of interaction that we found in later classes made it clear that we acted on our intentions to break the traditional pattern of classroom discourse. Instead of maintaining teacher dominance of the discourse, we used our power as teachers to structure and sequence class assignments and activities to encourage active student participation in classroom talk. Apparently, Helen's case analysis assignments worked extremely well as a means of changing the nature of classroom discourse. When David returned to her course during the fourth week of the semester, it was clear that Helen was not dominating class discussion. That is, as they discussed the current case narrative, Helen's students took over 90 percent of the conversation turns, had all twenty-three of the long turns, and spoke directly to each other in cross-talk 75 percent of the time.

David's attempts to break the usual pattern of teacher dominance in classroom discourse included class activities and discourse rules that directly required student participation. For example, in the second meeting of his class, David ensured that each of his twenty-six students spoke by having the students interview each other using a list of topics generated by the class and then introduce their partners to the whole class. In an interview shortly after this class session, David explained, "I thought it was only fair to show my students that this is not the kind of class where they can just sit back and say nothing." Throughout the semester, David used similar strategies to make students' active contributions to class discussion the norm. He, for example, regularly expected students to present possible thesis sentences to the class as a basis for discussing the feasibility of topics. This overt structuring—along with David's two-response rule—allowed students to take nearly two-thirds of the conversation turns and to speak to each other in cross-talk about one-fourth of the time. In addition, even David's long turns often functioned as invitations for students to comment further.

This analysis yields two observations that may be useful to other teachers who are attempting to engage their students in new speech genres for classroom discourse. First, it may be necessary to begin with some teacher-dominated discourse to set up the kinds of activities that will engage students more actively in knowledge making. Second, pedagogy that invites students to have a literal voice in knowledge making does not happen simply because a teacher announces that he or she desires it. Simply telling students that they will be engaged in such activities is not enough; teachers must deliberately set up class activities and assignments that put students in active roles as knowledge makers (more on this in chapter 3).

Controlling Classroom Tasks and Topics

Setting up the kinds of activities that prepare and encourage students to take active roles as knowledge makers is an important means of encouraging student participation within a general framework set up by the teacher. Of course, there is always the chance that such participation might erupt into free-for-alls or regress into teacher-dominated patterns unless new ways of interacting are developed. Within any given classroom, local speech genres thus need to be worked out that allow students room to explore connections between their experiences and disciplinary knowledge and that, at the same time, preserve the teacher's ability to shape the discussion when necessary.

Given that the previous analysis suggested that there was little room for lecture and IRE discussions in our class sessions, we next explored what sorts of interactions characterized the discourse. To accomplish this we used a coding system developed in the 1960s by Bellack, Kliebard, Hyman, and Smith that assesses how each conversation turn attempts to control the substance and pace of subsequent classroom discourse by identifying each turn as a structure, solicit, response, or reaction move. Structure moves are the most controlling in that they directly set up a task (e.g., "Let's discuss case B") or topic (e.g., "Let's talk about how the author balances the use of logos, ethos, and pathos in this piece") or manage turns (e.g., "Ann, and then Pete"). Solicit moves are the next most controlling because they usually introduce a task or topic with a question (e.g., "Was anyone else bothered by the lack of support for the claims in this paper?"). Response moves are the most controlled in that there must be some clear connection to a structure or solicit move (e.g., "He provided no evidence for his claim that the tuition hike is unjustified.") Finally, reaction moves are the least controlled and the least controlling in that they show no direct link to a previous structure or solicit move. Bellack and his colleagues used this coding system to show the traditional pattern of teacher control. Within this pattern, the tenth- and twelfth-grade teachers they studied controlled the basic flow of the class by using nearly all of the structure moves. In addition, the sequence of solicit, response, and reaction moves was much like what later researchers called the IRE pattern: teachers initiated topics with solicit moves, students responded, and teachers reacted with evaluations of the students' responses. Indeed, Bellack and his colleagues' use of this coding system was one of the principal influences in later classroom discourse research that identified the IRE pattern.

A more complete description of actual coding is included in the table on pages 42–43.

Table: Rules for Coding Conversation Turns

Move	Characteristics*	Qualifications	Example
Structure Turns (STR)	Speaker exercises control over task or topic, allots turns, makes meta-comment.	Teachers usually effect STR moves but students also can, can double as a solicit (SOL) [see below].	*David:* I'll tell you what, for the purposes of introduction, why don't you just pick a partner, and we'll see who someone who can't find a partner will have to be in a group of three. For the purposes of introduction, let's move the chairs around into a circle so we can see each other.
Solicit Turns (SOL)	Speaker exercises control over next conversation move, asks a question, or specifies a respondent.	Rhetorical questions are not always solicits. Tag questions commonly are solicits.	*Helen:* [writing on chalk board] The whole idea about universality, universal as opposed to social constructionist, well, it's not universal; it's relative, right?
Response Turns (RES)	Speaker's comments are an immediate result of a STR or SOL move; response can be verbal or nonverbal (laughter, silence).	There might be multiple RES to one STR or SOL. Speakers can structure their own STR or SOL and then respond immediately to it.	

Move	Characteristics*	Qualifications	Example
Delayed Response (DR)	Speaker's comments are a direct but not immediate result of a STR or SOL. Usually, the responding speaker signals that s/he is giving a delayed response by invoking the same language in the original response.	A DR is differentiated from being simply an additional RES to a STR or SOL by its being removed in time and sequence from the discussion right after its controlling STR or SOL.	Since RES, DR, and REA turns are understood contextually, examples are coded as part of the discourse sequence discussed in the example that follows.
Reaction Turns (REA)	Speaker's comments show no direct link to a previous STR or SOL.	A REA is the "default choice" in coding conversational turns.	

*Not all the characteristics noted above need be present for the turn to qualify as a given type of move.

In the example that follows, this coding system allowed us to sort out the extent to which Helen and her students shared control over individual tasks and over the introduction and elaboration of specific topics for discussion in this particular class session.[2]

95 (STR) *Helen:* Okay, how about case B?

96 (RES) [thirty-four seconds of silence as pages rustle]

97 (RES) *Tammy:* This is really interesting to me because as a TA in 500 [the proseminar for first-time teaching assistants] we're talking about teaching the writing process to our students in 104 and 105 [first-year composition classes]. And there are these steps, and we're all kind of saying, "Yeah, that's right,"

			and then we get into, "Wow, maybe that's not necessarily what's right" after reading the articles.
98	(REA)	*Class:*	[laughter, in response to Tammy's use of the word *right*]
99	(RES)	*Tammy:*	Right, or it's the *reality* of, and it was very interesting. I think we discovered that there were different theories. I knew there were the step, step, steps we learned in high school: first you do this and then you do this, and then you do this, and then you learn the recursive process, but now I find it's even more than that, and I was really kind of surprised, anyway.
100	(REA)		[twenty-eight seconds of silence]
101	(DR)	*Val:*	I guess what I found most interesting about case B was the issue of orality, of how important it is to talk about what you're writing about. I'm discovering this on my internship where the first task is to interview all these people about different programs. I have to write proposals and to find out what the programs are about, what's important to these people, and, you know, what they need money for and why, and all of that. So it's not like you go off in this vacuum and in a dark room and [chuckle] turn on your little light and sit at the computer screen and type up some sheets of paper. You really have to interact with people before you can even start writing. You have to enter the persona of the organization.

This example illustrates three ways that Helen and her students shared substantive control of the topics of discussion. First, although Helen's structure move does indicate her general control over the overarching task (to move the class from discussion of case A to discussion of case B), that structure move serves as invitation for her students to take the initiative in introducing topics that they wish to discuss. Thus, like the teachers in Bellack and his colleagues' study, Helen uses a structure move to control the basic task of the class, but that structure at the same time serves to limit her control of the topics for discussion within that basic task. This pattern of teacher-control of basic tasks but ceding of control of specific topics was consistent throughout the ten class sessions that we examined. As teachers, we took an overwhelming majority of the structure turns in the ten class sessions that we examined (David, 83 percent, and Helen, 66 percent). However, the majority of those turns were used either to set up class tasks in which students introduced the topics for discussion or to manage discussions by allotting turns.

The second point that this excerpt illustrates is that students often controlled the initiation and elaboration of topics. In turns 97 and 99, Tammy introduces an issue for discussion. The class's subsequent laughter seems to be an unsolicited reaction to Tammy's use of the word *right*. (Helen's class had a running joke about how nothing was ever "right" in the sense of there being an absolute truth in class discussion.) Turn 100, a twenty-six–second silence, shows a nonverbal reaction to Tammy's response; that is, the class decides not to pursue Tammy's topic further. Finally, in turn 101, Val clearly ties her delayed response to Helen's structure move by using language that echoes that move while introducing an alternative topic for discussion. A lengthy discussion of Val's topic then ensues.

This example is somewhat unusual in that both of the initiations of new topics are made in response moves. In our classes—as in the classes that Bellack and his colleagues studied—new topics usually (1) were directly introduced as questions via solicit moves (students had 40 percent of these moves in David's class and 48 percent in Helen's class) or (2) indirectly emerged as reaction moves during relatively unstructured conversation (students had 80 percent of the reaction moves in David's class and 90 percent in Helen's class). However, both of us used structure or solicit moves like

Helen's either to start a discussion or to revive a flagging discussion. For example, later in this class session when a long silence indicated that discussion was waning, Helen simply asked "Any other issues?" and then waited until a student initiated a new topic. Similarly David often used solicit moves to invite students to introduce new topics or extend the discussion of the current topic. For example, he'd ask "Other responses?" or "Do others of you agree or disagree with Diane's response?" to get students to continue discussions.

The third point that we draw from this example is that the discourse in classes clearly departed from the typical IRE pattern of interaction in which teachers strictly control both tasks and topics on a turn-by-turn basis. Had the discussion in Helen's class followed IRE, we might have expected Helen to react to Tammy's contribution with some kind of evaluation in turn 100. Instead, Helen declines to comment on Tammy's response, leading to a 26-second silence. This silence is broken when Val nominates a new topic for discussion. After this excerpt, the class moved into cross-talk for eighty turns in which the students explored the problem that Val raised, narrating similar experiences, asking devil's advocate questions, and raising issues from the theory articles that they had used to write their case analyses. Helen's silence in place of an evaluative comment (turn 100) thus allowed space for Val to make her delayed response, which then served to initiate the topic of class discussion for the next eighty turns. The lack of student response to Tammy's initiatory move versus the extended commentary elicited by Val's move essentially served as a type of peer evaluation on the importance of each respective student's nominated topics to the class as a whole.

In summary, then, the coding of our class transcripts suggested that, in terms of tasks and topics, moving away from traditional teacher-dominated speech genres does not mean that we as teachers abandoned all control over the basic tasks of our classes. However, while we retained overall control of the these tasks, we also asked relatively few questions and, when necessary, endured long silences to encourage students to gain and use initiation rights over both the tasks to be performed in the class and, especially, the topics of the class discussion. Certainly teachers cannot initiate all or nearly all of the topics for discussion (as is the case in lecture and IRE discussions) and expect that mutuality will develop. At the same time, teachers cannot abdicate their duty to represent disciplinary knowledge to their students (see Graff); school as an institution would be pointless if students didn't learn something that they didn't already know. Moving toward alternative speech genres for classroom discourse thus entails negotiating how teachers and students will share control of tasks and topics, as well as examining the question of the nature and extent of that sharing.

Reciprocity in Evaluation

Although students having the floor and gaining initiation rights are likely signs of movement toward alternative speech genres, teachers could still undermine such a move by dominating the evaluation that occurs. If teachers were to simply withhold evaluation only to impose it later in a class session, the opportunity for students to hold the floor in classroom discourse and to initiate and propagate new topics might amount to little more than giving students enough rope to hang themselves. Unless students also participate actively in the evaluations that occur in classroom discourse, true mutuality is unlikely to develop. Thus, we believe the extent to which there is reciprocity in evaluation among teachers and students is a critical test for the extent to which students and teachers are engaging in alternative speech genres and pedagogies.

The issue then becomes how much evaluation should there be and what is the desirable balance of teacher and student in this evaluation. In IRE discussions, teachers do nearly all of the evaluations, indicating the acceptability of students' responses about every third turn. This pattern of teacher control of what counts as knowledge involves little room for mutuality to develop. Clearly, the movement toward alternative speech genres and mutuality in the construction of knowledge is not likely unless the IRE pattern of teachers evaluating students' contributions about every third conversation turn is broken. Even so, it is also possible that a noticeable absence of evaluation from the teacher might leave students with a confused notion of what counted for knowledge and thereby undermine students' sense of themselves as knowers in relation to disciplinary knowledge. Thus, reciprocity in evaluation lies somewhere between the extremes of teachers doing all or nearly all of the evaluation and teachers doing none of the evaluation.

To examine the extent to which evaluation was reciprocal in our classes and the means by which we achieved or failed to achieve that reciprocity, we had to first identify each of the evaluative statements in the ten transcripts. To do so we began by distinguishing between implicit and explicit evaluations. Explicit evaluative moves were easier to identify because they made a clear positive or negative judgment about such things as a course reading, another student's contribution, a teacher's contribution, or the procedures informing the class as a whole. Implicit evaluations were more difficult and required careful attention to the context. For instance, in discussion of case B in one of Helen's classes, Val commented, "I guess what I found most interesting about um, case B, was the issue of orality, of how important it is to talk about what you're writing about." We counted this as an implicit evaluation of case B because the positive or negative nature of the term "interesting," used to evaluate the clutch of articles used as readings for case B, is open to interpretation. If, on the other hand, Val had said "I thought the readings for case B were excellent, because . . . ," there would be little if any doubt as to Val's stance, and her response would have been coded an explicit (and positive) evaluation of the course materials. We also noted whether the evaluation was positive, negative, or, in a few cases, simply an acknowledgment; who made the evaluation; and what was evaluated (e.g., students' or teachers' contributions, course readings, sample texts, or class procedures).[3]

Three clear patterns emerged from this analysis. First, evaluation was less frequent than would be expected in IRE discussions. In classes dominated by IRE discussion, about one in every three turns would include an evaluation. In David's undergraduate class, the ratio was about one in seven, and in Helen's graduate class the ratio was about one in six. These lower ratios are consistent with a pedagogical approach that delays evaluation to allow for continued discussion among participant-knowers. Second, students had the vast majority of the evaluations in both courses (about 65 percent in David's class and about 75 percent in Helen's class). Third, students' contributions were the objects of evaluation only about half of the time. In classes dominated by IRE discussion, we would expect students' contributions to be objects of nearly all of the evaluations. In our classes, other objects of evaluation included (in descending order of frequency) course readings, general items of world knowledge (usually occurring during the discussion of the undergraduates' papers), teachers' contributions, miscellaneous topics, class procedures, teachers' or students' own contributions, and communication theories (all of these occurred in the graduate class). Reciprocity is indicated here in that not only were students themselves evaluators but they also received considerable feedback about their contributions. Feedback about students' contributions came as part of a context in which many other things, including teachers' contributions, were also the objects of evaluation.

Examples drawn from one of David's class sessions illustrate how an initial move toward reciprocity in evaluation might take place. In this class session, David asked his students to discuss a sample paper written by a student in a previous section and then to discuss the preliminary oral plans presented by three of their current classmates. His purpose was to draw out his students' evaluations of the paper and plans to create a dialogue about what constitutes a good thesis statement that is well supported. He chose to engage his students in dialogue rather than simply pronounce judgment himself. In the examples that we have drawn from this class session, it is clear that the students were both direct and harsh when evaluating a less than perfect sample paper that was written by someone unknown to them. For example, during the discussion of the sample paper, T.J. called it "slop." Several students were more specific, commenting on lack of a discernable relationship between the writer's thesis sentence and his supporting material.

Pete: He didn't really support his thesis. [explicit, negative evaluation]

Laura: What is the thesis statement; what is the main point?
[implicit negative evaluation]
Mark: How come it doesn't, um, relate to his thesis? [implicit
negative evaluation]

Two points seem important here. First, David deferred evaluation of
this example to his students. His only evaluation in this part of the
discussion was to validate students' responses; for example, he directly affirms Mark's observation: "Okay, good question." Second,
the students are wholly negative in evaluating this faceless student's
work.

A few minutes later, David asked the class to respond to their
classmate Trent's oral proposal of a topic for a similar paper (that
"if people knew more about ozone depletion . . . they'd stop using
aerosol products"). Immediately, the evaluations became more polite. The first student's response to Trent's proposed thesis was negative, but the critique was implicit: "Do you think each person's
going to think that they can make a difference?" As discussion developed, Pete posed a direct critique of Trent's plan for a questionnaire but did so in the form of a question rather than a declarative
statement. Although the proportion of explicit and implicit evaluations in the two segments was about the same, there was a more
exploratory feel to the class's responses to Trent. Also, Trent was an
active participant in the process: he resisted Pete's point, and he
readily acceded to others, often using direct, one-word positive con-
firmations (e.g., "right," "yeah") to signal his assent. David, himself,
had a number of positive evaluations of students' evaluative contributions. For example, David acknowledged the complexity of
Trent's topic when the rest of the class seemed to be trying to over-
simplify it ("So this is a complex topic"); David also tried to get
Trent to see a classmate's point when Trent did not seem to accept
the evaluation being offered ("Pete makes a good point here").
While David's moves, then, were decidedly evaluative, they were di-
rected not at Trent's paper but at the evaluation strategies of the students commenting on that paper.

A closer look at the evaluation of students' contributions in both classes confirmed that this pattern of deference when evaluating the contributions of one's current peers was consistent in both classes. For example, a large proportion of students' contributions received positive teacher evaluations: David's ratio of positive to negative evaluations is almost three to one, and Helen's is almost seven to one. Further, David had only three explicit negative evaluations of students' contributions in five meetings of his class, and Helen had only one in the five meetings of her class. The teachers' evaluations thus were consistent with an approach in which participants were jointly making knowledge, rather than with a situation in which the teacher was the recognized guardian of received cultural knowledge. Students made almost twice as many evaluations of other students' contributions as did the teachers. In these evaluations, students also followed the pattern of being more direct (i.e., using explicit evaluation moves) when providing their peers with positive feedback and being less direct (i.e., using implicit evaluation moves) when providing negative feedback.

The analyses of how evaluation functions in these two very different classes suggest what might be taken as some basic ground rules for setting up reciprocity in evaluation:

- Teachers delay their feedback, often inviting students to give responses and later confirming what has been said.
- Participants may be direct in their criticisms of examples, course readings, class procedures, or their own contributions but usually buffer their criticisms of students' contributions.
- Evaluation is a mutual activity, with teachers commenting on students' contributions, students on each others' contributions, and students, albeit reservedly, on teachers' contributions.

The tendency toward delay and deference, reflected in these ground rules, did not eliminate feedback for students about their contributions. Evaluation was still integrated into the discourse and sometimes involved evaluations of evaluations. Moreover, the tendency toward deference also did not mean that feedback was always polite.

Summary of Speech Genre Analyses

In alternative pedagogies the relevant question is not "How does the teacher maintain authority and control?" but "How is control exercised by teachers and students alike?" and "How do both teachers and students assume knowledge-making positions in these classes?" Our exploration of the discourse in our classes suggested three tentative answers to these questions: (1) the pattern of teacher dominance of classroom discourse is broken so that students get literal voice, (2) students share control of the initiation and elaboration of topics, and (3) there is reciprocity in evaluation. Given the considerable differences between our classes, our observations about the commonalties that we observed might be taken as guides for others attempting to engage their students as knowledge makers in other settings. However, it must be remembered that alternative pedagogy, by definition, can exist only as teachers and students work out ways to share the making of knowledge. Indeed, rather than taking our observations as recipes for alternative pedagogy, we hope that other teachers will follow our lead and form partnerships to explore their own teaching. Doing so need not involve the elaborate audiotaping, transcribing, and coding that we did. Observations and running tallies of who gets to talk, when cross-talk breaks out, who initiates tasks and topics, and how evaluation is handled would likely suffice in most cases. However, doing these kinds of observations alone is almost impossible because demands of participating in classroom discourse may obscure a teacher's perception of the class. For example, after one of the class sessions that David observed, Helen came to her interview upset with herself for dominating the class discussion. She estimated that she'd taken about 50 percent of the conversation turns. When we analyzed the tape, we discovered that she was mistaken; her students had taken over 80 percent of the turns in that class session (in this instance, the case study students' estimates of her contributions were much more accurate). Apparently, her perception of the session was colored by one or two exchanges in which she felt she'd exercised too much control over the students' knowledge making, and she failed to see that her interventions were really exceptions to the overall pattern of students' active participation in knowledge making.

Implementing Alternative Speech Genres

Given the caveats just expressed about the situated nature of alternative pedagogy, we will hazard two more observations about the implementation of alternative speech genres. These observations are based on some further examples drawn from two of the class sessions that we observed and on the case studies that we conducted with students in each other's classes. The first point is that implementing alternative speech genres means that teachers must find strategies that both allow students space to explore their ideas and set reasonable expectations for students' and teachers' contributions. The second point is that teachers' attempts to implement alternative speech genres will not mean the same thing to all students. Because of differences in such factors as race, gender, class, ethnicity, and previous educational experiences, students will have differential responses to teachers' invitations to engage in knowledge making in classroom discourse. Some will enthusiastically accept such invitations, while others are likely to hang back.

Strategies for Implementing Alternative Speech Genres

Two important indications of the exploratory nature of the discourse in our courses were that relatively unstructured reaction moves dominated the discussion and that our students took the vast majority of these turns in cross-talk. Indeed, the most common mode of interaction in our classes was students speaking directly to each other in reaction moves. Critics of alternative pedagogy might argue that so much freedom in classroom discourse could lead to off-topic talk, confusion about what counted as knowledge, and even chaos. A closer look at the discourse in two of our class sessions suggests that we were not simply abdicating control; instead, we used a number of specific strategies to negotiate control of the discussion with our students. Again, the strategies that we illustrate in the following discussion should not be seen as a definitive list for alternative pedagogy; rather, these strategies are the techniques that emerged in our attempts to engage our students in alternative speech genres. They should be taken as possible starting points for teachers teaching in situations similar to ours.

1. *Teachers use structure and solicit moves to implement course architecture that invites students to take active roles in knowledge making.* A meeting of Helen's graduate class about two-thirds of the way through the semester best illustrates how this strategy can be applied. Nearly all of that class session was devoted to the discussion of case D. In this class session, Helen used only two overt structure moves. She used one to begin the class, asking the students whether they preferred to finish the discussion of case C (missed because the previous class was canceled due to Helen's illness) or move on to case D for which they had just prepared case analyses. The class chose to move on to case D. Four hundred sixty turns later, Helen used her second structure move, "Ah, why don't we turn these [the case analyses] in" to end the class session. In the vast majority of turns between these two structure moves, Helen's students held the floor. They were engaged in cross-talk 75 percent of the time and took 90 percent of the turns. Helen also used questions as her basic means of shaping the discussion. After the students decided to move to discussing case D, Helen implemented their decision with the following solicit move: "Okay, tell me about case D. [eight seconds of silence as pages turn] What were some of the issues that you identified?" In fact, Helen's invitations to nominate topics can be seen as a filament running through this class session, giving it a modicum of structure. When discussion flagged about one hundred turns into the discussion, Helen repeated her invitation: "Any other issues that came out as you were reading?" Near the end of class, she provided one more chance for students to nominate new topics: "Any last-minute issues that you want to bring up before you hand in these analyses?"

The sparseness of the guidance from Helen in this discussion must be seen as a function of the small class size, the educational experience of the graduate students, and the design of the course. That is, the cases, selected readings and materials, the description of the assignments that encouraged "no one right answer," and the case analyses themselves prepared the students to take active roles in class discussions. In contrast, David used more elaborate structure moves to set up class discussion to prepare students for the peer review session, the main business of a class meeting that occurred at about the same point in the semester. As the following excerpted lines illustrate, because of his larger class size, he also used questions to directly invite specific students to nominate topics for discussion.

403 *David:* We won't make Laura stop writing; we'll start with Travis.

413 *David:* And which category does that fit into?

415 *David:* What about yours, Marty?

2. Teachers endure long silences when necessary. In the two class sessions we have been discussing, silences lasting more than ten seconds were fairly common. Often these silences were the awkward sort of silences that teachers must learn to endure while students flip through their notes or review the reading to refresh their memories. These thoughtful moments stood in counterpoint to other instances in which students competed actively for the floor and were more often than not broken by a student rather than the teacher. Indeed, often during these silences, David could be seen silently tapping his foot, forcing himself to wait while his students gathered their thoughts.

3. Teachers use uptake to validate and invite elaboration on topics introduced by students. Both of us occasionally used what Nystrand and Gamoran call "uptake"—conversation turns in which teachers pick up on a topic mentioned by students and expand it in further discussion. In the excerpted lines that follow, Helen fills a break in the discussion with a conversation move that returns to a topic raised earlier by a student.

| 100 | *Helen:* | Well, Sam, since you brought this up, are you saying we have a definition of *professional* here that applies to professional writing? |
| 112 | *Helen:* | And how does that relate to what you were saying earlier, Karla, about, ah, interpreting context? |

Helen's use of uptake here differs from Nystrand and Gamoran's examples in that her uptakes are not immediate. In turn 100 she refers to a topic Sam unsuccessfully introduced ten turns earlier and in turn 112, to a topic Karla introduced twenty-nine turns earlier. Also, Helen's use of these uptakes clearly invites specific students to comment in more depth rather than serving as an opportunity for Helen herself to provide the elaboration as the uptakes might have if they had come in the evaluation slot of an IRE exchange.

4. *Teachers encourage students to elaborate with direct or indirect affirmations.* Frequently, David used direct questions that asked for clarification from the topic proposers and questions that invited respondents to comment further (e.g., "Why do you say that, Craig?"). He also combined uptake of students' comments on problem statements with invitations for the original proposers to comment further (e.g., "What do you think about what Pete was saying, Laura?"). In contrast, Helen's affirmation of students' contributions was usually less direct. Although Helen took relatively few turns in the long discussion during her class session, she made it clear that she was actively listening to her students by using simple affirmations that encouraged them to keep talking. For example, when Val stumbled over a detail ("the Borg study?") in her recounting of an issue, Helen reassured her with a simple "uh-huh" that is voiced loudly enough for the entire class to hear. Through the long discussion, Helen stepped in several times with a short "um-hum," "uh-huh," or "okay" that indicated both her attention to the speaker and encouragement for the speaker to continue.

5. *Teachers ask real questions.* Authentic questions, Nystrand and Gamoran's term for questions that actually function to prompt or acknowledge knowledge making in students, are rare in traditional classroom discourse. That is, in traditional classrooms, teach-

ers use questions to initiate the topics that they want to focus the class discussion around. In discussions governed by IRE-style discussion, teachers pose questions, not because they are interested in discovering what the student is going to say but because they want to know whether the student knows the "correct answer." Teachers' questions served very different functions in our classes: our questions invited students to nominate topics or encouraged students to explain their positions further or to clarify and challenge positions taken by others.

The use of authentic questions does not mean that teachers never use questions to pursue their agendas for learning. For example, David asked the following question to get the class to consider how Julie's proposed problem statement could be revised to serve a different purpose: "Well, Julie's at kind of a formative stage here. Let's try to write her three different [problem statements], one for each of the categories. What would a thesis be for the 'there is a problem that exists'" [category from Flower's textbook *Problem Solving Strategies for Writing*]? David's intent here is clear: he wants the class to get some practice seeing how stating problems differently can affect the development of a paper. His question is an implicit structuring move (changing the class's task from reporting which category each student's problem statement best fits to exploring alternative ways of stating problems). The question also includes an implied evaluation ("Julie's at kind of a formative stage"). Yet, the resultant discussion makes it clear that the students knew that David did not have a single answer in mind. In fact, it became the class's job to help Julie develop some new possibilities.

Helen also occasionally used questions to press her own agenda. For example, during a discussion about whether common knowledge of the type presumed in speech act theory exists, Helen made the following statement: "I'll give you an example. What does my husband mean when he comes in and says there's dust on the fireplace mantle?" Here, Helen is fairly direct in announcing that she is giving the class an example to consider; she is pressing an agenda. The resultant discussion makes it clear that her students knew that there was not a single answer to this question. In fact, one of her students remarked, to the great amusement of the class, "It means that he wants a dust rag," even though the majority opinion was that Helen's husband was implying negligence in her housekeeping. Helen's example worked because (1) it invited different responses and (2) the similarities and divergences in the responses illustrated that the commonalties often assumed in speech act theory are not absolute.

Several times during this class session (as in the example that follows), Helen also made what could have been seen as a fairly definitive claim but softened her statement by adding a tag question at the end to invite exploration of theoretical issues.

182	(SOL)	*Helen:*	So, really, this is information . . .
183	(RES)	*Sandy:*	Yeah.
184	(SOL)	*Helen:*	. . . in the sense that it might be information for Borg, right?
185	(RES)	*Class:*	[laughter]

Such exploration was in line with her agenda of helping students recognize theoretical issues and stances in professional communication.

6. Teachers make direct interventions in class discussion. Although the dominant pattern in both of these class sessions was for students to explore their ideas in cross-talk, we, as teachers, did make direct interventions when we thought it was appropriate, although David did so more often than Helen. For example, about halfway through the discussion of case D, Helen took the initiative by summarizing and refocusing the previous discussion:

This is interesting because what you have, on the one hand, is a speech act assumption [with underlying] dimensions and the assumption that certain things have a basic standard value, certain genres. But on the other hand, Karla is saying that, that all of these are affected by interpretation and the situation. So how can there really be a perlocutionary act?

Later in the class, Helen also introduced an example from research and a personal example that she pursued for several turns.

Similarly, after the peer review session in his class, David intervened with a structure move, "Okay, let's circle," to bring the class back together. Then, he led a discussion of several students' topics, again focusing first on which of the three categories students' problem statements fit into. Like Helen, David invited students to nominate the actual topics for discussion (their problem statements); however, David exercised direct control in choosing which students presented their topics and in focusing the discussion on determining the type of the problem statement.

After discussion of several students' problem statements, David intervened yet again to change the nature of the task when it was Julie's turn to share her topic. However, to curtail his dominance of the discussion, David invoked his two-response rule to encourage cross-talk. Later, David tried to get the class to see that Julie's problem statement could be written to meet each of the textbook's categories. In the next sixty-eight turns, he used solicit moves to force the class to discuss how changing Julie's problem statement to fit each of the three categories would affect the development of her paper. Students engaged in cross-talk during much of this discussion, but David clearly exercised control of the pace and direction of the discussion. David ended the discussion of Julie's topic after Laura concluded that changing the type of problem statement also changed the audience for whom Julie would be writing. David seized this segue to audience analysis by asking whether any of the other groups had an interesting discussion of audience analysis that they would like to share with the class.

In summary, then, the examples of these two class sessions illustrate that attempts to change the nature of classroom discourse to achieve mutuality must be implemented turn by turn with the students. The form such efforts take will likely vary according to situational variables and the repertoire of class management strategies that a teacher sees as useful in a given situation to convince their students that they are really expected to take active roles in the making of knowledge.

Students' Responses to Alternative Speech Genres

Assuming that engaging classes in new speech genres provides the same opportunities for all students to contribute to knowledge making would be naive because changes in discourse patterns will not automatically erase social and cultural differences. Instead, we must see the speech genres of classroom discourse as intimately bound up in the subjectivities of the students and teachers involved. As feminist theorist Chris Weedon explains: "Social relations, which are always relations of power and powerlessness between different subject positions, will determine the range of forms of subjectivity immediately open to any individual on the basis of gender, race, class, age and cultural background" (95). A student's response to a teacher's invitation to engage actively in knowledge making in classroom discourse will depend on (1) that student's socially constructed subjectivity and (2) the resultant perception of roles open to that student.

To explore how differences in students' subjectivities affected their participation in alternative speech genres, we conducted case studies with two students in each class. Case study students were selected on the basis of their responses to a questionnaire, given on the first day of class, dealing with students' comfort in contributing to class discussion and desire for teacher control of class talk and activities. The observer for that class (not the teacher) read the questionnaires and identified several students who scored on either end of the spectrum of responses to teacher authority. From these lists, we each chose two students who were willing and able to participate (several students from David's class were not able to commit to the series of five interviews because of work schedules).

In the discussion that follows, we focus on Sam and Penny, the case study participants in Helen's class, because the most dramatic difference in subjectivities emerged between them. Sam, the only male in Helen's class, was clearly comfortable from the outset with Helen's plan to engage students actively as knowledge makers. In an interview after the first meeting of the class, Sam explained:

Helen I see functioning as a facilitator and gatekeeper to make sure we're going somewhere. But it's really the interaction between the students that is going to be the, you know, hashing out the ideas and challenging each other. You know, I don't see her standing up there and lecturing.

At the time of the study, Sam was a first-semester student in the rhetoric and composition masters program; he had a B.S. in computer science and had done master's-level work in computer science and speech communications. Even though Helen's course was his first in his current master's program, he immediately saw how his background in communication theory would be relevant, and he was already planning to go on for a Ph.D. in rhetoric and professional communication. In short, from the outset, Sam saw himself as joining a new academic community, and he also saw his previous educational background as relevant to the current class, wondering whether the "theory underlying composition matched his background in '70s speech communication theory." Thus, he found it easy to accept Helen's class as a situation in which learning would occur not with Helen delivering lectures but with the class participants hashing out ideas and "challenging each other," and he saw himself as an active participant in that process.

In contrast to Sam's initial view of the course, Penny's was much more hesitant. In her interview with David after the first class meeting, Penny was candid about her concerns:

> I was warned about this class—mainly the teaching style— from friends who know me well. I'm really a structure person, and I prefer to have pretty definite guidelines [so] that I can take my notes and they're organized. And [I prefer] that the instructor is organized. When it's real loose, that frustrates me.

At the time of this study, Penny was in her second semester of course work toward a master's degree in rhetoric and professional communication and had worked as a registered nurse for several years. Unlike Sam's, Penny's initial view of herself as a contributor to knowledge was much more limited. Given her background in nursing rather than English, Penny felt that she would have to prepare extremely well for class discussions and she would not contribute to the discussion of articles that she had not read carefully. She explained to David that she would contribute only when she had something "intelligent" to say, and, by implication, she felt she probably would not be able to contribute that often. Unlike Sam, Penny did not anticipate that her past academic work had sufficiently prepared her in any way for this current course.

Early in the course, the difference between Sam's and Penny's initial responses to the course seemed to hold: Sam seemed completely comfortable with students doing most of the talking in class, while Penny wished Helen would guide the class more. For example, Sam commented after the second observed class session, "What seems to be working particularly well is that Helen doesn't say a whole lot. You know, there was the one point in the class where she asked the question, and the silence; she just waited until someone answered."

In contrast, Penny's favorite part of that same class session was when Helen engaged in a variant of an IRE exchange with her. In a delayed response to Helen's question about whether expressivists buy into a Cartesian dichotomy between inside and outside, self and other, Penny unwittingly suggested that she herself bought into the Cartesian dichotomy (see turn 239 in the example that follows). Helen's reaction to Penny's response came in three parts. First, (in turn 240) she simply repeated a part of Penny's point to clarify whether that's what Penny had meant and to see whether any of the other students had a comment about Penny's observation. Then, after a seven-second silence, Helen provided an indirect evaluation of Penny's contribution (turn 242) to which Penny immediate assented. Finally, Helen (turn 244) explored the significance of Penny's making the dichotomy of self-other in terms of expressivism. Penny had originally explained that expressivism denied the dichotomy of self-other based on the idea that the self is all.

239 *Penny:*   I think more, just more the inner, not so much the outer? You know what I mean? It, it's everything from within. It doesn't matter what the rest of the world

thinks. It just, um, I don't know how to say it. It doesn't matter so much what the rest of the world thinks, just to express yourself is the most important thing.

240 *Helen:* Basing everything from within; it doesn't matter what the rest of the world thinks.

241 *Class:* [seven-second silence]

242 *Helen:* You just made the dichotomy.

243 *Penny:* Oh, Okay. Yeah, yeah.

242 *Helen:* If that's the way we define expressivism: we look to ourselves. The truth is not out there somewhere, and we're just having perceptual difficulty. The truth's in here.

Sam and Penny's responses to this unusual exertion of authority by Helen illustrate the differences in their initial responses to her pedagogy. When David showed the excerpt to Sam, Sam saw this exchange as Helen using her teacherly authority in the service of fomenting student agency: "trying to get conversation going" rather than "fishing necessarily for a specific answer." In contrast, Penny saw the excerpt as Helen finally giving her some much needed direction: "Any direction that she would offer—I was thrilled!"

Despite these rather dramatic differences in their initial responses to the class and their perceptions of their roles in the class, Sam and Penny participated about the same amount in class discussion in the five classes that David observed. Neither spoke as much as several of the Ph.D. students who, at times, dominated the class discussion, but neither was as silent as several of the other masters students in the class. Also, as Penny became more comfortable with Helen's approach during the semester, Sam and Penny's views about value of the class discussions became much more similar. Eventually Penny came to trust that Helen really believed in class discussion and that she was not one of those teachers who allowed the class to make "stabs in the dark" when they "have no idea what direction the instructor is trying to lead the discussion." Instead, both Sam and Penny reported that one of Helen's primary roles was summary and occasionally moving the class away from a "circular" or unproductive discussion.

By the end of the course Sam and Penny shared many views about the value of students' contributions to discussion and Helen's limited interventions, and both were convinced that the real work of building knowledge happened as students discussed the course readings, the case narratives, and their own experiences. However, their descriptions of those discussions were not identical. Sam saw the class as "hashing it out." For him, one of the most important features of the class discussion was that the participants could engage in critical exchanges without becoming adversarial. He cited an example of a student correcting him without making him feel uncomfortable. He explained that two of the students—Rachel and Cynthia—also would "get into it, playing off each other with no residual effect." He also reported playing devil's advocate himself at times. For Sam, these critical but safe exchanges were evidence of the class's growing coherence and sense of trust.

In contrast, Penny described the class discussions as making knowledge at the dinner table. She explained:

> I don't think that anything that anybody really says in the class isn't valued. Nobody really seems to judge you on your comment, but they may help you re-steer, or not even so much re-steer, but just keep taking it, you know, further. You just wait 'til there's a pause and kind of jump in and say it.

Penny was equally clear that this cooperative discourse did not eliminate differences. Some of the participants were more knowledgeable in terms of communication theory and some in terms of relevant workplace experience: "They are more articulate and maybe a bit stronger on where they are standing." Like Sam, Penny identified Rachel and Cynthia as more confrontational than the rest of the class members, but she saw the class not only as cooperative but as "mothering": "whenever anyone is stuck, somebody always comes right in and fills in."

It is tempting to read these two cases solely in terms of gender. Certainly, gender does seem to explain some of the differences between Sam and Penny. Not surprisingly, Sam is more willing to see himself as a knowledge maker than Penny is, and he emphasized productive conflict in the class discussions while Penny emphasized cooperation. However, it's equally true that two of the women in the class were the most aggressive contributors to knowledge and the most willing to engage in substantive conflict. These cases make more sense when gender and previous educational experiences are considered together: Sam is male and had relevant educational background; Penny is female and was socialized as a nurse to expect knowledge to be organized and codified. Rachel and Cynthia are women, had considerable academic and workplace experience, and had been socialized in other graduate seminars to speak their minds actively. Our point here is that no single factor such as gender, race, ethnicity, sexual orientation, or previous educational experience can completely predict how a student will participate in alternative speech genres. Although Penny's gender was likely a factor in her original choice of nursing as a profession, her educational experiences in nursing (she was expected to learn bodies of information and to take orders without question from doctors) reinforced her perception of herself as recipient rather than a producer of knowledge. From our perspective, the most exciting aspect of Penny's case is that the class discussions she participated in helped her to see a new role for herself as a contributor to knowledge.

Mutuality in Knowledge Making and Discourse Relations

Fundamental to our argument in this chapter has been the notion that subjectivity—the ability to see oneself as a knowledge maker—exists only in discursive practices. Further, the discursive practices of the classroom greatly effect what kinds of subject positions students are able to take. When we review the analyses in this chapter, several things seem clear. First, student participation is fundamental to learning and meaning making. However, the degree to which students are engaged in classroom discourse depends, to a large extent, on how teachers exercise their considerable authority. Second, creating mutuality with students involves creating discourse patterns in which students have voice, can use their voices to speak to each other directly, and have a reciprocal relationship with teachers in determining what counts as knowledge through evaluation. Finally, teachers can use their authority to create opportunities for students to express agency in classroom discourse, but students' responses to such invitations to take subject positions as knowledge makers will vary depending on such things as age, previous educational experiences, and gender.

All of this leads us to raise the point of postmodern feminist theorist Chris Weedon that the "individual is never in a state of innocence when faced by a choice of conflicting subject positions" (97). All of the participants in our classes had agendas that affected the subject positions that each was able or willing to take. Clearly, our choice as teachers to engage our students in alternative forms of classroom discourse had the greatest effect on what subject positions were taken. Ironically, we also saw that choice as constraining the exercise of our teacherly authority, and our own subject positions were further defined and, to some extent, limited by the amount and kinds of agency our students were willing to engage in. For their part, our students (taken as groups) seem to have embraced our invitations to take new subject positions, although we suspect that some did so reluctantly.

Finally, we want to again emphasize that we do not hold up our classes, the ways in which we engaged our students to create mutuality, or the subject positions we and our students took in these courses as definitive of alternative pedagogy. Rather, we see the contribution so far as illustrating Weedon's point: "Different discourses provide for a range of modes of subjectivity and the ways in which particular discourses constitute subjectivity have implications for the process of reproducing or contesting power relations" (92). The crux of the issue of subjectivity in classroom discourse then becomes not what kind of pedagogy is traditional or alternative, paternalistic or feminist, modernist or postmodern, right or wrong, but whether or not the assumed naturalness of the subject positions inherent in the traditional patterns of lecture and IRE-style discussion is called into question. Whether or not teachers engage in alternative pedagogy, we believe that they are morally enjoined to consider what subject-object positions their pedagogy imposes on students or invites their students to take.

For teachers and students engaging in alternative pedagogy, participating in classrooms calls for a new set of competencies. Hull, Rose, Fraser, and Castellano remark that competence in classrooms in general means "interactional competence as well as competence with written language: knowing when and how and with whom to speak and act in order to create and display knowledge." Competence in alternative classrooms adds a layer of complexity. In alternative pedagogies, traditional competencies, such as knowing when and how to respond in an IRE framework, must be augmented and, often, replaced, by new competencies, involving when and how to respond in a framework featuring mutuality in knowledge making and reciprocity in evaluation. In this chapter, we have argued that one area of competency in the alternative classroom is the ability to participate in new classroom speech genres that overturn traditional subject-object relations. In the next chapter, we discuss how the interaction represented by these new classroom speech genres can become part of an overall course architecture that plans for and promotes mutuality among classroom participants. Being able to design and implement such course architecture is a second major area of competency for those engaged in alternative pedagogies.

3 / Course Architecture and Mutuality in Student Writing

> [A]s long as we do not engage in critique and correction of the curriculum, the framework of meaning behind particular questions of what to teach to whom will continue to prove inhospitable to all those who have been excluded from knowledge and knowledge making.
>
> —Elizabeth Kamarck Minnich,
> *Transforming Knowledge*

> [T]he educational practice of a progressive option will never be anything but an adventure in unveiling.
>
> —Paolo Freire,
> *Pedagogy of Hope*

In this chapter, we argue that mutuality in student writing depends on transforming course architecture. We defined *course architecture* in chapter 1 as the management of assignments and activities that make up the day-to-day procedural functioning of the class and, in particular, the ways in which classroom assignments and activities encourage or discourage interaction among disciplinary knowledge and students' varied knowledge and experiences. This chapter extends that definition. On one level, course architecture is curriculum. As Minnich points out in her epigraph, curriculum serves as a "framework of meaning" in American classrooms, and this framework has traditionally been exclusive rather than inclusive. Minnich also reminds us that we must recognize "the intimate intertwinings of sex/gender, class, and race in the history of education as in all else" (11–12). But, achieving a curriculum that is inclusive in terms of subject matter, of ways of thinking, and of gender, race, and class cannot be effected easily. It cannot be effected, for example, by simply inviting marginalized groups to participate in class discussion or by taking a "noncanonical approach" to course content. Similarly, achieving a course architecture that is inclusive in who gets to make knowledge in the composition classroom involves more than just saying that we are committed to mutuality in student writing. It cannot be effected by simply adding peer review to our writing classes or by adding multicultural readings. Designing a course architecture that enables mutuality in student writing involves nothing less than overcoming the implicit, pervasive exclusion of students from knowledge making in traditional American educational practice. Course architecture designed for mutuality is the structure that enables new classroom speech genres (chapter 2) and interpretive agency (chapter 4) to permeate classroom business.

Course architecture is also what Freire in his epigraph calls "an adventure in unveiling" (Hope 7). It is dynamic rather than static. As an ongoing process, a course architecture that pursues mutuality has qualities that are similar to Freire's concept of *conscientizacao*, or critical consciousness. Victor Villanueva defines critical consciousness as "the ability to see the dialectical relation between the self and society" and argues that the process Freire refers to begins with the "private, lived experience" but expands to include the interaction with the dominant culture (Villanueva, 477).[1] In the composition classroom, the value of "private, lived experience" has sometimes been translated as expressivist approaches to teaching writing. Such approaches are embodied in Elbow's statement, "But damn it, I want my first-year students to be saying in their writing, 'Listen to me, I have something to tell you' not 'Is this okay. Will you accept this?'" (82). Correspondingly, interaction with dominant culture has entailed attention to disciplinary discourses, as reflected in Bartholomae's position: "there is no writing that is writing without teachers . . . there is no writing done in the academy that is not academic writing. To hide the teacher is to hide the traces of power, tradition, and authority present at the scene of writing" ("Writing" 63). A course architecture striving for mutuality in student writing will naturally reflect the tension between personal experience and disciplinary knowledge embodied in the positions of Elbow and Bartholomae.

Indeed, course architecture that attempts mutuality in student writing is necessarily affected by students' past interactions with disciplinary discourses and the "relations of power and powerlessness between different subject positions" that are embodied in knowing, or not knowing, conventions of academic writing (Weedon 95). When mutuality is the goal, a teacher's job is to create a course architecture that allows for a variety of useful intersections between students' varied abilities as writers and the abilities and conventions valued in academic disciplines. Mutuality in student writing exists only as such intersections are continually recreated.[2] The challenge that we turn to in this chapter is how to foster these intersections through course design.

We do not claim to have a magic formula for designing and implementing course architectures that create mutuality in student writing. Instead, we offer three principles and illustrate what it means to implement these guidelines with examples from our own teaching. Course architecture that encourages mutuality

- allows teachers and students to share agency in the design of writing assignments
- includes writing activities that bring together students' knowledge and experiences with specific disciplinary representations of knowledge
- harnesses the power inherent in teacher's evaluative roles in the service of encouraging students' interpretive agency in classroom discourse and agency as writers.

In discussing these principles, we see the move toward mutuality in student writing as linked to opportunities built into the architecture of writing courses.

Sharing Agency in the Design of Writing Assignments

In the design of writing assignments, sharing agency with students means that teachers must consider how to negotiate three important aspects:

- how acceptable genres will be defined
- how representations of disciplinary (as well as other kinds) of knowledge will be brought to bear
- what roles will be available to teachers and students

Often, first-year college writing courses are focused on expository genres that are selected and defined by the teacher. Teachers exercise control over how disciplinary knowledge is represented by specifying features of the genres that must be used (even when students are allowed to choose their own topics), by selecting the readings to which they must respond, and by selecting other materials that, implicitly or explicitly, further conventions of academic discourse. Students find their agency as writers limited to fulfilling as best they can the assignment as explained by the teacher and to helping other students figure out how to do the same. In pedagogies striving for mutuality, teachers may still exercise a modicum of control over these aspects of writing assignments. Indeed, the examples in this section—David's starting points, Helen's case analyses, and Helen's magazine assignment—illustrate that teachers may focus on negotiating only one or two of these aspects in the service of creating mutuality. What is important here is breaking the usual pattern in which teachers control every aspect of the assignment and enabling negotiation of genre, content, and roles.

Negotiating Genres in Starting Points

In many college writing courses, teachers plan a sequence of writing assignments that they hope will build students' analytical skills and will help students to see differences between genres. For example, at our university, the suggested syllabus for the second-semester first-year writing course begins with a summary assignment, moves to a short argument paper, followed by a rhetorical analysis, and concludes with some type of longer research paper. The rationale here is that students need to demonstrate that they can represent others' arguments fairly and can make their own limited arguments before they move on to the more difficult genres of rhetorical analysis and of extended argument with researched support. This approach assumes that a teacher can predict in advance the set of writing experiences that will benefit students. The "starting points" example that we examine here puts up for negotiation both the substance and the sequence of the genres that students will write.

Starting points are writing prompts based on issues that have evolved from class discussion of the assigned readings or from examples of student writing. David developed the starting point approach to writing assignments because he wanted to invite his students to help him expand the range of genres that would be acceptable beyond the expository assignments that he usually taught. In addition, the starting points approach allows David's students to have, through journal entries and class discussions, some input into how disciplinary knowledge affects their writing. This approach also allows students to take a modest role in controlling their writing tasks in that they decide which of the starting points they will respond to.

The starting point we examine here sets up two options for writing and illustrates two ways that students' expressions of agency can be built into that aspect of course architecture that deals with assignment design. First, this starting point shows student input by using a statement from a student's (Jamie's) journal as the catalyst for the option of "Tracing Your Heritage."

> *Tracing Your Heritage Option*: In her journal response to the Walker reading, Jamie argued that the critical line is "Guided by my heritage of a love of beauty and a respect for strength—in search of my mother's garden, I found my own." Jamie argues that in this statement, Walker reveals that her primary purpose in writing this piece was not to tell "us about the experiences of those women just so we, as readers, would be more cultured"; rather, Walker wrote it for her own benefit: "I saw this piece as more of an entry into the diary of Alice Walker rather than into the fourth edition of the English text *Ways of Reading*."

To ground a second option, "Understanding Difference," the starting point uses the class's shocked response to Harriett Jacobs' "Inci-
dents in the Life of a Slave Girl."

> *Understanding Difference Option*: Several of you expressed
> shock and surprise at the descriptions of the treatment of
> slaves in Jacob's "Incidents in the Life of a Slave Girl."
> From our [the class's voiced] perspective, it seems unusual
> that such things could possibly have happened, and yet
> thousands of people owned slaves and probably relied on
> justifications similar to the ones that Dr. Flint gave to
> Jacobs.

Not only does student input inform the topic options, but students' preferences also dictate the genres for writing about these
topics. For "Tracing Your Heritage," students are invited to "Write
a piece in which you attempt the same two tasks; that is, investigate
some aspect of your heritage as a way of showing your own connections to your parents, grandparents, or other important people of
another generation in your life." Here, the genre negotiation is implicit; no genre is specified. Students are simply admonished to
show "connections to your parents, grandparents, or other important people of another generation," and to "provide enough details
so that we begin to understand more about the life of the person(s)
who you focus on." For "Understanding Difference," students may
"[w]rite a piece where you consider some aspect of Jacobs' story
from the perspective of one of the other characters." Here, the negotiation of genres is explicit; students are directly invited to "mix
narration and exposition" as Jacobs did. The architecture of David's
course encouraged students to read these instructions as an implicit
invitation to define the genre as they saw fit through previous examples of mixed genres. David began the course by using a series
of model academic and professional texts to illustrate how published writers often intermingle narration, description, and exposition.
Then, in the class discussion of Walker's text, students identified

specific places where Walker used narration, description, and exposition for various purposes.

This starting points example illustrates that attempting to create mutuality in class assignments does not necessarily mean ceding complete control to students. Although David explicitly invited his students to select options and to define genres for their own writing, he clearly exercised considerable control of the representations of disciplinary knowledge in that he chose the narrative-descriptive-expository focus and the texts that served as models for the students' writing and to which the students had to respond.[3] David also retained considerable control in that he wrote all of the starting points. Students exercised agency as writers in that they could write in response to one or neither of the offered starting points. In the next example, Helen defines and enforces an expository genre but allows her students more leeway in determining what disciplinary representations of knowledge are relevant.

Negotiating Content in Case Analyses

In writing courses, genre knowledge is a common form of disciplinary knowledge. But disciplinary knowledge can and does take other forms in the rhetoric and composition classroom. In Helen's graduate course, for example, such disciplinary knowledge is represented by theoretical approaches to and current research in the field of professional communication. The case analysis assignment illustrates her attempts to directly negotiate that content knowledge within the framework of a strictly defined genre. The case analyses governed the first half of the graduate course, and their purpose was to encourage students to make connections between personal experience and disciplinary knowledge. As such, the assignments demonstrated that such invitations can mean different things to different students. Before class discussion of a given case, the students were required to write a case analysis that discusses a case narrative, its supporting materials, and some of the article-length pieces included in the course pack. (Excerpts from the oral discussions have already been included in chap. 2.) The syllabus specifies the genre constraints for the analyses, requiring that the analyses contain

- a list of the primary and secondary issues *you* find in the case (please word these as issues and not as topics)
- a brief explanation of how the *primary issue* is evident in the case
- a short theoretical discussion that examines how the primary issue has been addressed in various required readings (include at least two or three required readings in your discussion)
- a short application of the theoretical discussion (above) to material(s) included for discussion at the end of the case.

The syllabus also specifies format, recommending headings, subheadings, and formal documentation. Helen reinforces these constraints under "submission requirements," in which the syllabus reminds students to check "that you have the four required sections" and reviews what those sections should be. Helen further enforces adherence to this genre by refusing to grade any case analyses that do not include the required elements, and she spends long hours in one-on-one conferences with students who have trouble understanding how to revise their case analyses to meet the aspects of this genre that she sees as critical. Thus, Helen strictly controls the case analysis genre.

When considered in terms of overall course architecture, however, the case analysis assignment embodies the opportunity students have to take subject positions in this class, even given precisely defined assignment criteria. In fact, Helen enforces the genre to help students see that there is no one right representation of disciplinary knowledge and to prepare students to actively participate in the reconstruction of disciplinary knowledge in class discussion and in later written assignments. For example, although the listing of issues is required, the syllabus emphasizes that "the *primary issue* is the one issue that you have selected to be your main focus" and that "your *primary issue* is the issue, large or small, that interests you the most or that you feel most confident in discussing." Clearly, Helen has an agenda in this assignment that reflects her understanding of the reading, writing, and thinking skills the graduate students must have if they are to do well in the discipline they are trying to enter. Yet, it is also clear that Helen expects her students to exercise considerable control over their analyses and to bring their personal thinking and experiences to bear on the disciplinary content as represented by the case narrative and readings. Indeed, two aspects of the design of the assignment make it impossible for students to turn the case analyses into a find-the-teacher's-answers task. First, each case includes more readings (about ten) than any one student could include in his or her analysis, thus inviting students to choose readings they find most relevant to the issues. Second, the syllabus explicitly notes that students' primary issues will differ and that there is no one "right answer" to be found. The refusal of "the right answer" encourages students to act as subjects in this assignment, as well as in subsequent team-project and individual-essay assignments, which seek connections between the students' experiences and academic knowledge.

When designing a course architecture that operates at the intersection of disciplinary knowledge and students' experiences in negotiating course content, teachers must keep in mind that students' unique subjectivities will affect the degree to which each individual writer might assume authority in his or her own writing. Indeed, when we looked at the interviews of Sam and Penny, the two case study participants from Helen's class, we saw that they began the course with very different perceptions of themselves as writers and knowers. Sam saw his undergraduate background in communication theory and graduate education experience in computer science as a good basis for this communication theory course, and his initial survey also indicated comfort with active student participation in class discussion. Penny saw her nursing background as providing little basis for this course, and her initial survey indicated comfort with teachers who very clearly control what counts as knowledge in class discussions and activities. Given this initial contrast, we wanted to examine how these differences might "determine the range of forms of subjectivity immediately open to any individual" (Weedon 95).

Both Sam and Penny held potentially contradictory views of themselves as knowers. Sam's view of himself was mixed: because of his past graduate experience in speech communication, he was confident that he could critique theory and build knowledge, yet he was keenly aware that he was new to the discipline of rhetoric and professional communication. Thus, Sam expressed genuine surprise that he was getting A's on his written case analyses when some of the other students with backgrounds that were precisely germane to the course were not getting grades at all until they revised. Unlike Sam, Penny did not, at least initially, view herself as a knower and did not anticipate that her past academic work in nursing had sufficiently prepared her in any way for her current course of study. As the class progressed, Penny's view of herself came to reflect a tension between this initial insecurity and her growing confidence. While her writing established her competence as a knower—she received A−'s and B+'s on her analyses, she attributed this success to checking her case analyses against those written by a friend in a previous section. And, while she did not look at his case analyses before she wrote hers, "because it's such a discovery process that it would just ruin what you're supposed to get out of it," she still felt the need to check her discoveries against another student's before she came to class.

Although Sam and Penny reached similar points in their development as academic writers in Helen's class, the paths that they took to those points differed. Their separate responses to Helen's invitations to mutuality in their writing remind us that when mutuality is the goal, relevance must not be defined solely in terms of presumed monolithic disciplinary standards that all students must meet. Instead, relevance entails heterogeneous subjectivities and must occur at the intersection of each student's previous knowledge and ongoing experience with new material.

Negotiating Roles in a Magazine Assignment

In the first two examples we have examined, sharing agency in the design of writing assignments meant primarily the direct negotiation of genres with students (starting points) or the direct negotiation of representations of knowledge (case analyses). In both, the roles that students played were still mostly prescribed by the teacher.

This third example entails an assignment that features the direct negotiation of students' writerly roles. Helen's magazine assignment places first-year writing students in editorial teams to produce a class magazine as their writing for the semester. Published two times during the semester, the magazine features a range of student writing, including essays, analyses, interviews with a narrative frame, and book and media reviews. Each issue of the magazine has two sections. The two sections allow students to hold staff-type roles, such as editor, designer, or producer, for one section and to be a writer-contributor for the other.

The assignment requires that Helen cede considerable control in all three aspects of agency in the design of writing assignments. Students decide what genres they will write and what textbook and other readings they will use as models for their writing. Students also define their own roles as writers and editors. The discussion that follows illustrates how Helen sets up this active negotiation of students' roles as writers and editors and how allowing her students such direct agency limited her ability to introduce a new concern of her own. Students thus take on roles both as someone who gets to exercise control over what kinds of writing will be considered acceptable and as someone who must meet the expectations for writing set up by others. As editors, students choose a general theme for their section, specify genres, and set up guidelines for submissions. As contributors, students select the specific topics they write on, given the guidelines set forth by the magazine staff for their section. In one issue, for example, staff members of one section requested pieces following the general theme of "music," while the staff for the second section asked for contributions that represented different genres, such as personal experience narratives, news reports, features, and reviews. Students signed up to write pieces that the student staff was soliciting. The only teacher-driven stipulation was that class members had to submit at least five to seven pages of approved text for each issue (the text to be edited by peer reviewers, revised by the contributor, and approved by the magazine staff).

Although Helen cedes considerable control to her students in this approach, she does not simply leave her students to teach themselves. She provides a course pack with instructional support to help students understand new genres, writing techniques, and effective peer review strategies. Yet even these instructional materials are negotiated in that it is entirely up to students to decide whether this information is useful and how to use it. Because the magazine assignment informs the students' writing for the bulk of the semester, negotiating tasks, topics, and writerly roles becomes an ingrained part of the subjectivity of many of the students in Helen's first-year classes. Students are invited to take direct control of their own writing and of the writing of others—unusual roles in most school settings.

Ironically, and perhaps necessarily, this sense of being in charge generated resistance to an end-of-the-semester assignment that Helen gave in one such class in which she tried to reassert traditional teacherly authority in a writing assignment (an assignment that she subsequently changed in light of this experience). After her students had published their magazines, Helen asked them to revise one of their pieces so that it followed a traditional academic claim structure. She began this assignment with a brief minilecture, using a handout to explain how to structure major and minor claims in a line of argument (e.g., how to write topic and subtopic sentences that developed a single thesis). Her students, who had come to identify success in writing in terms of the self-defined genres, resisted her attempt to move them toward this more traditional academic structure.

One student, who had effectively chronicled in her magazine contribution the unfortunate personal experiences and important musical achievements of rapper Tupac Shakur, responded to the revision assignment by focusing on development. She proposed to add more detail about "how Tupac has helped the youth of today and about the projects he was recently doing" and about "how upset Tupac was growing up fatherless, but how in the last few years he met and got to know his father." The student explained that this detail didn't show up in her original article, because, "I didn't want to stray too far from the editor's call for articles on 'current events.'" In omitting changes in claim structure from her plans, the student implicitly expressed continued satisfaction with her ideas in their current narrative organization.

In response, Helen remarked that the student's revision plan did not seem to address the assigned task of revising for academic claim-support structures and asked the student to follow more closely the organizational advice in the handout. After the student made several unsuccessful attempts to do so, Helen finally suggested that she construct a single paragraph from the original narrative using a traditional academic claim-support structure. In response, the student composed the claim "Tupac was looked up to by youth for surviving a rough childhood" and wrote

> Tupac was called a gangsta rapper by critics, because of his explicit lyrics and his violent history. But to his fans, Tupac was a rap artist who could put reality into rhythm and song and make a person sympathize with his situation or connect the meaning of their own struggles to his. To Tupac's fans, he was like a guiding light, a man who had suffered many of the hardships and troubles of everyday youth. From selling drugs to living in poverty, being fatherless, and [having] a parent on drugs, he showed he could survive. For the youth of today, he was a sign that they could suffer and struggle and still be successful in life. His early lyrics were full of much hate, but as he grew in his career, and change could be noted in his music. . . . [Quotes from Tupac's rap songs complete the paragraph.][4]

The fact that this student did not explicitly include in this paragraph the claim she had worked so hard to construct demonstrates how irrelevant the academic claim exercise was for her. In addition, the fact that this paragraph, unlike her original narrative, was perilously close to plagiarism reinforced the sense that the student had lost control of her work. The student's resistance also suggests that, after having experienced success in her original way of writing about the material, she saw no good reason to change its organization just to suit academic discourse conventions. This example exemplifies the strong degree of authority a student writer can assume if personal experience—including in-class experience—has encouraged the student to assume subject status.

The examples that we've examined in this section illustrate that there are multiple ways to share agency with students in the design of writing assignments. The examples make it clear that teachers must carefully consider the extent to which they will negotiate genres with students, invite students to influence what representations of disciplinary and other knowledge will be enforced, and allow students to define their own roles as writers. As the Tupac instance suggests, once agency is ceded by a teacher it may not be easily reclaimed.

Pursuing Mutuality in Writing Activities

Creating mutuality in writing assignments is intimately related to attempts to create mutuality in class activities that support these assignments. In this section, we use examples from our classes to explore this interplay. One example involves peer review in David's original first-year writing class and the other, class discussion from Helen's graduate class.

Peer Review and the Commitment to Negotiation

Our example of Helen's magazine assignment noted how negotiation could be built into course assignments. The example of peer review session that we've chosen shows that such negotiation can be both explicit, in the case of students negotiating textual choices, and implicit, in the case of students overriding the teacher's instructions in their groups. In this example, David used terms from the textbook to frame the peer review task. When David then asked students what moving from "writer-based prose" to "reader-based prose" meant, students first parroted the textbook (e.g., "that there's no hidden logic") but, when pressed to say what the terms meant, fell silent. One honest soul finally admitted, "I don't know, but it's on page 190." With a series of pointed questions, David then elicited from the class a list of criteria that was to govern the peer review for "reader-based prose," often stepping in to reshape students' contributions before placing them on the list he wrote on the chalkboard. Although David worked hard to translate the textbook concepts into terms that made sense to his students, there's little evidence of mutuality at this point.

When we reviewed the audiotapes of peer review sessions of the two case study participants, however, we discovered that both Ann and Laura had ignored the list of criteria that David worked so hard to put on the board. Each focused instead on much more specific problems that they saw in their peers' papers. In doing so, both women exhibited considerable skill in getting their partners to understand problems in their textual choices. For example, Laura got Marty to listen to his own text and identify a repetition problem for himself.

Laura: Pretend it's not your paper, okay? Uh [reading from Marty's draft], the possible solutions to the garbage crisis are, recycling more than we throw away, building more trash incinerators, and creating less garbage are the best answers to the problem of what to do with Americans' abundant garbage.
Marty: I kind of repeat it twice.
Laura: Um-hum, yeah.

Ann displayed even more skill in getting her partner, Mark, to understand the problems in his draft and see ways to address those problems. The transcript makes it clear that Ann not only saw herself as capable of identifying problems but proved tenacious in the face of Mark's defensiveness regarding why he needed to address his reluctance to include his own opinions in the piece. In the excerpt below Mark responded to Ann's observation that he needed to "involve your quotes more in what you're writing about." Ann allowed Mark to voice his opinion before nailing home the point she was trying to make.

Mark: See, what I was trying to do was just get the fact here. I didn't want to really put my opinion into it; I just wanted

the facts. That's the way I wrote this paper. You know what
I mean?

Ann: Yeah.

Mark: Kind of like that fire engine one—that paper on the
problem analysis, I was trying to just go with mine. But I
thought about it and my opinion, like you said it is, and I
thought, "Well, if I just stay with the fact and I don't put
my opinion in . . . "

Ann: Okay.

Mark: I can't go wrong.

Ann: What you still need to do is you can put your opinion in,
or at least [use] words like I said, the January thing for
Newsweek, you know, that way you can kind of blend it
together instead of just saying oh this and this and this.

Given Mark's adversarial reputation in the course and his defensiveness about Ann's suggestions, Ann's performance in this session is remarkable both for its restraint and its persistence. Apparently, Mark had overreacted to David's comments on his last paper
and removed all of his own opinion from this one, hoping that simply sticking to the "facts" would keep him out of trouble. Not only
did Ann see herself as able to identify problems in Mark's text, but she
also achieved what David could not in the opening segment. She
found language that identified a specific problem in Mark's text ("you
can't go at it one-sided, but you can put your opinion in here") and
then negotiated language with him to help him understand how to
change the problem ("blending" quotes with his own opinions).

The mutuality that emerged in these peer review sessions seems
to have developed despite David's attempts to impose a particular
set of disciplinary concerns on the students. As such, the first-year
students' agency in this example stands in contrast to the agency
built into the magazine assignment discussed earlier, in which negotiation of writerly tasks and roles was built into the syllabus.
Here, there was "silent negotiation" of the assigned task. The question of why this negotiation occurred gets to the heart of how course
architecture works.

We see three possible aspects of David's course architecture that enabled Ann and Laura's departure from instructions. First, although David attempted to impose a set of criteria on the class, he was not as prescriptive as he could have been. He might have prepared a peer review work sheet that listed the criteria and forced the students to respond to specific prompts as they read their peers' texts. But he did not, and the structure of the assignment thus left some room for student agency. Second, the peer review assignment occurred within an overall framework favoring student input. Thus, it's possible that the general pattern of openness to students' ideas in classroom discourse that we saw in chapter 2 carried over into this event. Students may have tacitly realized that they were free to do as they saw fit despite David's instructions, because the overall pattern of interaction in the class invited student contributions. Third, the peer review assignment took place in a class that had encouraged students to take subject positions. Ann and Laura clearly saw themselves as capable collaborators, as able to identify specific problems and propose appropriate solutions. It is also important to acknowledge that, as revealed in their interviews with Helen, Ann and Laura both entered David's course having confidence as subject knowers, each basing their confidence on prior experience. Ann clearly saw herself as a full-fledged knower from the outset, indicating a good match between her previous experiences with writing courses and David's class. Ann viewed herself as a better than average writer. She commented in one of her interviews that the "six little things" that David required with each of the writing assignments were often "busy work" for her; although she might do some of those prewriting activities in her head, she didn't need to write them down as required. She conceded, however, that some of the activities might be useful to other students. Laura similarly entered David's class with confidence in herself as a knower, but her confidence was primarily based on her real-world experiences. An important difference that Laura saw between herself and many other students was her ability to decenter from her own perspective and see other points of view. Laura also noted that, as a returning adult student, she had difficulty relating to topics like underage drinking and that most of the younger students had similar difficulties understanding her topics that involved workplace experiences.

Class Discussion and the Commitment to Collaborative Meaning Making

As we saw earlier in this chapter, the case analyses in Helen's graduate class prepared students for class discussion by requiring them to identify what they, personally, saw as the relevant issues in the cases and to bring disciplinary knowledge to bear in their analyses. Undoubtedly, this preparation contributed heavily to the active student participation in knowledge making that we saw when we examined patterns of classroom discourse in chapter 2. A question that remains about these assignments, however, is how they worked in the overall architecture of the course to help the students develop as writers. Here, the answer seems to be that the writerly agency Helen forced her students to take in their case analyses provided the basis for them to actively reconstruct disciplinary knowledge in terms of their own and their peers' perceptions and experiences.

One way that these discussions worked to develop students as writers was to help them see how interaction with others can help them push their own analyses further. Given that the students were required to commit to their issues in writing before class discussions, we might have expected them to defend their ideas in the subsequent oral discussion, perhaps looking to convince Helen of the value of their claims before she graded their case analyses. Surprisingly, this rarely happened in the class sessions that we examined. Rather, students tended to use their understandings to contribute to the knowledge being made as a result of the communicative interaction in the class. For example, Karla's written analysis for case D maintained that issues involving reader and writer purposes were central to the case. Using her prior experience with disciplinary writing, Karla framed her statement of issues with the kind of literary reference valued in her previous literature courses:

Through the Looking Glass by Lewis Carroll contains an interesting line in which one of the characters tells Alice, "what I tell you three times is true." If truth could be defined that easily outside of Wonderland, I'd have no reason to ask any questions. I could simply keep repeating myself. But, as case D illustrates, "truth" or "knowledge" is more complex than the simple repetition of facts. Each technician, working from the same set of titration value data, communicates a different message, a different truth, to the reader. This leads me to my *primary question:* How might different writer and reader purposes impact each "message"?

Similarly, Penny reflected her background as a registered nurse in her concern for professional standards as her primary issue for case D. In addition, her articulation of gender among her secondary issues drew upon her status and experience as a nurse practicing in a specialized unit dominated by male doctors, a situation that she had fully described in gender-related terms during previous oral discussion.

The *primary issue* in case D is "How important is it to follow standard business conventions?" Closely related are these questions: If each industry has its own set of conventions, how do writers learn these different norms? How does a writer address a reader from a different community with different assumptions?
Secondary issues are as follows:

- How important is persona to business writing? Can writers master different writing personas? How do writers know which persona to use in any given situation?
- Is there such a thing as male writing and female writing or even androgynous writing? Assuming there are different types, should writers be expected to use all types fluently? Do industries value these types differently? Should they?

The claims that Helen forced the students to identify in their written case analyses served as openers for oral discussion that made the differences in ways both Karla and Penny (as well as their classmates) interpreted meaning in the case. Students used oral discussions to collaboratively extend and revise the ideas that they had committed to in their individual analyses.

During discussion, for example, Karla did not cite or promote her own claims when responding to her classmates' comments. Karla responded to Val's observation that, despite politeness strategies, the case memos written by the male technicians seemed more confrontational than those written by the female technicians, by pursuing Val's issues, although implicitly disagreeing with a gender-based approach: "I wonder that if the name Mark hadn't been there, I would have read the memo and determined it was a woman writer, because it was so cooperative, you know: 'let's look at this and let's work this out. . . . '" Penny also did not promote her own claims, even though gender concerns informed one of her secondary issues (above). Penny essentially agreed with Karla, remarking that Mark's memo seemed "overly polite." In short, students collaboratively contributed to knowledge making during discussion by building on others' work, rather than by duplicating their own.

Furthermore, students used the oral discussion as a prompt to change their own identification of issues as being primary or secondary. For example, Rachel had listed issues involving status and power, as well as issues concerning objectivity in scientific discourse, collaboration in technical writing, and mentoring for newly hired writers within business and industry, as most important in her written analysis. Yet she identifies an issue as "most prominent" during class discussion that does not explicitly appear in her written list of primary and secondary issues: "Anyway, I thought, the issue that I saw as most prominent in the case is "What is my personal context? Should I be concerned just about my day-to-day job and not concerned about the whole company? Am I trying to build animosity or am I going for progress?" Of course, the different mix of students in each class in which Helen uses the case analyses causes the nature of these collaborative constructions of knowledge to differ somewhat. For example, the next time Helen taught this graduate course, the gender mix was more balanced, and a couple of outspoken male students were more aggressive about pursuing their own ideas. Yet, despite these variations in nature of the interaction, the dominant pattern seems to be collaborative exploration. In fact, a common reaction among students after class discussions is "Well, if I were to write my analysis now, it would be completely different." Thus, while the written analyses encouraged students to operate as individual subject knowers drawing on their past experiences, the discussion saw them operating as collaborative knowers, constructing knowledge in the situated social setting of the classroom.

Evaluation and Students' Agency as Writers

In chapter 2 we argued that teachers' attempts to create mutuality in classroom discourse by engaging students in new speech genres could be undermined if they did not also invite students to participate actively in evaluation of what counts as knowledge. In other words, teachers' invitations for students to actively join them in knowledge making would mean little if teachers, after waiting for students to weigh into a discussion, later pronounced judgment about which contributions were acceptable. The same danger lurks as teachers try to create mutuality in student writing because most writing teachers are required to assign grades that evaluate students' performance as writers. Indeed, Bleich (*Double*) sees grades as such a threat to teacher-student reciprocity that he refuses to give them.

We believe that Bleich's position is too extreme. Certainly, teachers' evaluations of students' writing represent a possible threat to the development of mutuality and may also valorize traditional notions of what it means to master disciplinary knowledge. Yet, teachers' evaluations can also represent a creative tension between individual experience and social expectations in classrooms where mutuality informs writerly activities. For example, the mutuality that we saw develop in Helen's graduate class in chapter 2 depended, in part, on her insistence that the students' case analyses meet certain expectations for defining and analyzing issues. The reading, thinking, and writing skills that Helen demanded prepared students to contribute to the construction of knowledge in class discussion and in later writing projects in the course. In effect, Helen has a no-failure policy for the case analyses because she refuses to grade any submissions that are not at least attempting the types of analysis she expects and then works in individual conferences with students who need help until they see what kind of work they need to do.[5]

Teacher evaluations and even grades themselves can serve as an integral part of creating mutuality in student writing in that they provide occasions for teachers and students to negotiate what are acceptable contributions to disciplinary knowledge as it is continually being reconstructed in classrooms. Balance is critical. In the evaluation of students' writing, the trick in creating mutuality is to walk a careful line between total abdication of responsibility (i.e., "anything goes") and absolute control that reduces student agency to guessing what the teacher wants. Of course, there is not one right answer for how teachers and students should strike this balance.

The following example from one of David's first-year writing courses explores ways to engage students in dialogue about the meaning and application of evaluation criteria. The contract system we discuss here shows how such dialogue can be built into the evaluation component architecture of a course. After David began using starting points in his first-year college writing courses, he also began using a type of contract system in grading to try to focus the evaluation process more on improving students' writing than on justifying a grade. In this contract system, students can revise and resubmit a paper as many times as they like. Each submission receives one of three evaluations: continue revising (for submitting any reasonable draft), satisfactory (for a solid, well-developed paper), or outstanding (for really excellent work). Students submit between four and six different papers, and their top four evaluations make up the majority of the their final grade. For example, to pass the course (get a C–), a student could submit as few as four papers that received "continue revising" evaluations. Students get agency in this system in that they choose which of their papers to spend time and effort revising.

Even though this contract system gives students some control of how they expend their effort, the system in and of itself does not invite students to negotiate evaluation criteria. To create such dialogue, David requires that each submitted paper have a writer's memo and a peer's advocacy statement attached. In the writer's memo, students identify any important audience assumptions, evaluate the strengths and weaknesses of their own papers, and make an argument for the overall evaluation that they believed their paper should receive (see Jeffrey Sommers's discussion of writers memos for a more complete description). In the advocacy statements, peers evaluate the paper, make suggestions for changes, and argue for what they see as an appropriate evaluation. Although David clearly remains in control of the final adjudication of the evaluation, his responses are constrained and shaped by the students' writers' memos and advocacy statements.

The following excerpts show how writers' memos and advocacy statements represent teacher-student negotiation of evaluation. David's student, Jane, wrote about her experiences involved in moving and changing schools a number of times for a paper entitled "The New Girl." The writer's memo that accompanied Jane's second submission of the paper revealed what she saw as the strengths and weaknesses of her current draft:

> I feel the beginning does a great job of grabbing the reader's attention. The sequence of events helps to keep the paper flowing as the reader moves through my first day of school—from my introduction, to lunch, to P.E., and to the walk home. I also like the sentences at the conclusion of a few of the paragraphs; for example, "Nobody wants to eat with the new person on the first day" . . . I may have to add a few sensory details. I would like to develop the feeling of fear I felt on my first day. I also have concerns that the band paragraph is too braggy.

The advocacy statement, written by Suzanne, affirmed and added to Jane's statement of strengths:

> Jane's experience begins with an attention-grabbing intro which alludes to Jane's theme—what it's like to be an outsider . . . The reader gets a very clear idea of sequence through the use of words like "then," "next," and "after lunch." Jane's use of description (type of day, desk she sat in, what was for lunch) also provides a clear picture of the setting . . . The theme was effectively stated in one sentence at the bottom of the first page—"It is a terrible thing to be lonely."

Suzanne tackled the issue of weaknesses by suggesting where details could be added, such as what instrument Jane played in the band, where dialogue would contribute to the picture Jane is constructing, and where variety in sentence structure would help her presentation. At the same time, she assured David that Jane's draft currently met the criteria for the assignment. In short, by articulating strengths and weaknesses, students conveyed the grounds on which they believed Jane's text should be evaluated.

The following excerpt from David's evaluation of the paper illustrates interplay between the recommendations made in Suzanne's statements and David's own suggestions for improvement on a subsequent draft:

> I think Suzanne's right about your needing to split the band and choir paragraphs. And there are aspects of the band paragraph that I liked better in the previous version—that sense that even though you knew you were better, you were worried that the teacher would move you into Beth's chair too soon. That's a real piece of junior high, too. I think Suzanne is also right that the last paragraph, particularly the last sentence, doesn't work very well. It reads too much like those morals at the end of Sunday School paper stories.

David also agreed with Suzanne's assessment that Jane's draft was not yet "outstanding" and should retain its "satisfactory" rating. Although the decision rested with David, evaluation became the subject of dialogue, rather than monologue. For example, when Jane submitted the next version of this piece, Suzanne argued for an "outstanding" rating and placed considerable pressure on David to articulate specific reasons for why he believed the paper still deserved only a "satisfactory" rating.

In the example of Jane's paper, we saw a fairly cooperative process in which there was some disagreement among the three participants but in which the student writer, peer evaluator, and teacher seemed to be working together to improve the student's paper. It would be unrealistic to expect such seemingly wholehearted cooperation to occur in every case. In fact, teachers must expect that course architectures that enable mutuality will also enable resistance. Our next example shows how this resistance can take place within the context of evaluation. We conclude the analyses in this chapter with the case of Jack, a student in one of David's recent first-year writing courses, to illustrate how student resistance can emerge in evaluation and dialogue and the important role it can play in determining what kinds of revisions are necessary for a student to earn a given evaluation.

We pick up the story just after midterm. Jack, a 19-year-old agricultural studies major, struck David as wholly engaged in the business of the course yet resisting some aspects of it. Jack's journal responses to the readings were timely but were among the shortest in the class. Like many of his classmates, Jack also seemed a bit skeptical about the course readings. For example, in a discussion of Freire's critique of the banking concept of education (*Oppressed* 52–67), Jack brought up his meat-grading course as an example of a situation in which banking seemed an appropriate teaching method. After all, Jack reasoned that his professor knew the details of meat grading, and Jack simply needed the information presented to him so that he could learn it as well. Jack's example led to a good class discussion about situations in which banking approaches to learning might be appropriate, with most arguing for the banking approach in math, chemistry, and meat-grading courses.

Although Jack was not among the strongest writers in the class, he was clearly the most tenacious. By midterm, he had submitted his first paper, about his first experience seeing homeless people, four times and still had not secured a satisfactory evaluation. In a journal entry, Jack expressed resistance to David's comments:

> On my first paper I used the word *beggar* and I felt that this word expressed how I would recognize that person. But instead you told me to use the word *panhandler* because it would be more social correct. Well I think that being social correct is not always right because one thing that might be correct to one may not be to another. I'm not trying to give you a hard time here but you asked for our opinion.

In his response to Jack's journal, David wrote: "Yes, I did [ask for your opinion], Jack, and you're right to push me. In the larger scheme of things it doesn't matter much if you use *beggar* or *panhandler* in your papers. I just want you to know what most academic readers would think."

The choice between *beggar* and *panhandler* was symptomatic of a larger issue that Jack and David faced. Simply put, even though David changed his course assignments to represent a broader range of academic discourse, he still found himself wanting Jack to write like a middle-class academic. For example, the kinds of changes that David asked Jack to make in his original version extended far beyond word choice. One issue that emerged was the amount and relevance of the details that Jack included in his paper. In the original version of the paper about seeing panhandlers in the big-city mall, Jack began with two paragraphs about his small-town background, his father's change of job, and his parents' current marital difficulties. David's initial response to Jack's paper suggested that he "reduce the information in first two paragraphs into about half of the space" and then follow the advice of Mark, the student who wrote an advocacy statement for him, by trying to include more details relevant to the story itself. However, with the exception of a few small changes, these paragraphs remained essentially the same in the second version, while Jack added little detail to the parts of the story that David thought needed to be better developed.

David's response to the second version again was an attempt to convince Jack to reduce the information in the first two paragraphs:

> I still think that the first two paragraphs get into too much detail because that detail isn't directly related to the point of the story. I'd like to see you start with something more dramatic and more relevant to the story. Perhaps you could describe some of the big-city sights. Give us a sense of your 12-year-old wide-eyed wonder. That would set up a nice contrast with seeing panhandlers for the first time and would identify you as a small-town person without having to directly pound that into the reader's mind.

In the third version of the paper, Jack simply lopped off the first two paragraphs and started with his story. His brief self-evaluation suggests that he was simply trying to give David what he was asking for: "I think that the changes I have made are close to what you are looking for. I feel that the advice you gave we about taking off the top half of the paper was a great idea." Jack seemed to have simplified David's advice; apparently he saw the sense in eliminating the unnecessary detail but not the need to create the "wide-eyed wonder effect." Thus, in responding to this revision, David was faced with a choice of either sticking to his guns and demanding more detail or accepting Jack's simpler solution. David's decision, in part, acceded to Mark, who argued in his advocacy statement for this third version: "This is almost like a new paper. You have really changed the beginning, and I think it flows a lot better." David ended up accepting Jack's changes for the introduction but holding out for some minor revisions later in the paper before giving Jack a satisfactory evaluation:

I admire your persistence on this piece, and like both you and Mark, I think you've made a considerable improvement by cutting all of the explanation and just getting to the story itself. It hadn't occurred to me that you didn't even need to explain that your small-town experience was in Iowa and your big-city experience in Wichita. It's really not necessary. With the few small changes that I've suggested, I think that part of the story works well now and is satisfactory. However, later in the paper . . .

Overall, there's evidence that mutuality emerged during this interaction at least in part because of Jack's open resistance to David's attempt to get him to change his paper. David got Jack to do some of the things that he saw as necessary in this text, and helped by Mark, Jack got David to accept simpler revisions than the ones proposed. Perhaps the most interesting observation is that Jack's resistance seems to have served the same function as Jane's cooperation in the sense that both evoked further articulation with David about what changes were needed in the respective papers, but Jack's resistance also made the negotiation of agency more readily apparent. Indeed, after asking Jack's permission, David has used Jack's drafts and the accompanying memos to invite subsequent students to actively resist his attempts to shape their writing.

In focusing on David's contract and negotiation system of evaluation, we don't mean to suggest that it is the optimal way to create mutuality in the evaluation of student writing. Instead, we contend that teachers must consider how to address the difficult issue of evaluating students' writing while also trying to foster their sense of agency as writers. Nor is the way that a teacher decides to approach the evaluation of student writing the only issue to consider in course architecture that seeks to create mutuality. The more important issue is considering how the approach to evaluation will dovetail with other aspects of course architecture. As we have already seen, Helen often uses a traditional approach to evaluating her students' case analyses to enforce a particular genre in the service of creating mutuality in another aspect of her graduate courses. In the case analyses, any attempts to negotiate the genre are post hoc, occurring only when Helen meets individually with students who may convince her to read their texts differently. In contrast, David's evaluation procedure sets up the dialogue up front and allows students to take the first word in the evaluation dialogue even though he reserves that last word for himself. The value of this contract system is that it makes revision and dialogue about evaluation a normal part of the architecture of a writing class. In retrospect, we suspect that Helen's difficulty in the first-year class in which she tried to impose a traditional academic structure on the writer of the Tupac paper and her classmates was that she tried to change the rules of the game too late. That is, after committing to a course architecture that so clearly invited her students to take agency in defining their roles as writers and the genres they would write, she discovered that students resisted her imposing a specified genre on them at the end of the semester, because such a requirement, in effect, revoked the agency that had been so carefully designed into the course and that they had learned to employ and enjoy.

Welcoming Resistance and Seeking Transformation

As teachers trying to engage our students in alternative pedagogies, we must admit that we find it easier to deal with students whose beliefs about teaching and learning and whose previous educational experiences have led them to welcome the kinds of classes that we have designed. Such students may be ready, even eager, to take up roles as knowledge makers and to critically examine, even resist, the implications of disciplinary knowledge for them personally. However, we also acknowledge that we must welcome students' resistance to our own pedagogies, and we think it's important not to dismiss such resistance as the student's failure (cf. Segal's "discourse of failure"). Indeed, we recognize that we need to begin with a good-faith assumption that if students are reluctant to participate, it is not necessarily because they are incapable, shy, or unprepared.

As Fishman and McCarthy warn, students at times are wary of expressing divergent opinions because of a desire to protect social relations, rather than because of an inability to think critically.

Welcoming student resistance means little unless we as teachers are also actively seeking transformation of our own perceptions of what genres are acceptable in academic writing and what kinds of representations of knowledge are relevant in our classrooms. In this sense, student resistance might well lead to fruitful changes in the teacher's design of an assignment or of evaluation criteria that will benefit all classroom participants. Such change reflects mutuality between student and teacher where, as David Bleich argues, authority is redistributed: "the activity of students learning continues to be predicated on teachers teaching, but 'students learning' also comes to mean 'students teaching,' and 'teachers teaching' comes to mean 'teachers learning'" (*Double*, 253).

In this chapter, we have exemplified ways that students might be given opportunities to seek connections between the academic and personal, provide input into the definition of writing assignments, negotiate writerly roles and in-class activities, contribute to collaborative meaning making, and participate in evaluation. Depending on the design of the course, such opportunities can occur in both class assignments and activities. In addition, such opportunities, if designed with mutuality in mind, will feature new classroom speech genres (chapter 2), as well as interpretive agency (chapter 4), as integral architectural components. But even as we build into our courses opportunities for students to achieve mutuality, we must remember that we are "teaching against the grain."[6] As Minnich cautions

> It is certainly not crystalline clarity, not consistency, nor avoidance of contradictions that has held the dominant system in its place for so long; power, exercised and suffered directly through acts of exclusion, internalized in a sense of entitlement in some, in a sense of vulnerability or inadequacy in many others, is at play here. (180)

If all student writers are to participate in knowledge making in the composition classroom and beyond, there must be a transformation in the architecture of our courses. There must be a transformation in how the assignments and activities, classroom talk, and students' interpretive agencies work together in a composition class to encourage and enable inclusion.

4 Interpretive Agency and Mutuality in Classroom Knowledge Making: Or, Should David Have Told His Story?

When I assert myself aggressively, I feel as if I am imposing my authority on students, turning them into passive receivers of intellectual bank deposits. But when I hold back, I feel I am defaulting on my responsibilities, and I wonder what I am doing teaching at all. Pardon the sexist language, but in the one case I feel like a bully, in the other like a wimp.

—Gerald Graff,
"A Pedgogy of Counterauthority"

Since perplexity is necessary for learning, lecture is called into question because it is an effort to deliver solutions to problems owned by others. That is, unless students themselves own the problems and actively explore them, solutions lack significance. . . . [I]nstructor and students should engage in cooperative inquiry so that they alternate roles, becoming sufficiently sensitive to one another's contributions that they develop common understanding.

—Stephen M. Fishman and Lucille Parkinson McCarthy,
"Teaching for Student Change"

The epigraphs above embody the tension between a teacher's need to represent disciplinary knowledge, thus challenging students to think in new ways, and his or her need to enable a learning environment where students' contributions count as knowledge and where students, drawing upon their current competencies, ground new understandings in past and present experiences. Gerald Graff's epigraph suggests that school does not make much sense as an institution if teachers are stripped of disciplinary authority. Graff seems to reify disciplinary knowledge as the source of authority for knowledge making in the classroom (184). But to maintain that the authority to make knowledge in the classroom rests solely on disciplinary knowledge (or the lack thereof) means that the roles open to teachers and students are limited to teachers being subjects and students, objects. In contrast, Fishman and McCarthy, like Dewey, believe that knowledge "cannot be passed from teacher to student 'like bricks'" (346; see also Dewey, *Democracy* 4). They believe that education should focus on "the development of certain habits and dispositions rather than on the acquisition of a fixed body of knowledge" (346). Like Fishman and McCarthy, we believe that students should be actively engaged in the construction of knowledge. We also believe that fomenting student's interpretive agency is a critical component in creating mutuality because it is a first step in breaking the teacher-as-subject and student-as-object roles of traditional education.

Our emphasis on interpretive agency, in fact, reflects a model of learning that differs from those that underlie both the Graff and Fishman-McCarthy positions. Graff's approach privileges the transmission of knowledge to students; thus, interpretive agency is, at best, something to be carefully controlled and channeled into what the teacher sees as appropriate disciplinary concerns and, at worst, something to be discouraged and avoided. For Fishman and McCarthy, learning is transactional, and students' interpretive agency is seen as fundamental to the construction of knowledge in classroom discourse. Yet, Fishman and McCarthy advise that the teacher should set the "the conditions for student ownership and perplexity" or, in our terms, that expressions of students' interpretive agency must be limited to the kinds of contributions that the teacher sees as appropriate "cooperative inquiry" (352). For Fishman and McCarthy, students' interpretive agency must, at least to some extent, be limited and controlled. We believe that for mutuality to obtain in pedagogy, learning must be seen as transformational for both students and teachers, and that the expression of students' interpretive agency must be, at least to some degree, uncontrollable by the teacher and will be perhaps even dangerous at times.

We don't mean to imply that pedagogies that achieve mutuality will never include elements where teachers attempt to transmit knowledge to students. Nor do we think that teachers should set up transactional exchanges in the classroom simply to expose differences in students' subjectivities. Instead, we recognize that engaging students' interpretive agency may involve not only classroom business in which teachers express considerable control but also exchanges in which teachers cannot and probably should not ensure that students are safe from conflict. Transformational pedagogy requires that the expression of student agency extend beyond simply valuing students' contributions to including those contributions in the construction of knowledge at any given point. The emergence of mutuality, in fact, depends on an overall pattern of classroom interaction in which students' contributions become regular parts of the speech genres that characterize a class and on a recasting of the roles that students take in the construction and negotiation of the assignments and activities that constitute the framework of meaning or course architecture of a writing course.[1]

The purpose of this chapter is to illustrate how actively inviting students to bring their interpretive agencies to bear in the classroom can both enrich and complicate the process of constructing knowledge. We ground our exploration of interpretive agency here in the work of philosopher Donald Davidson. Davidson's theory of communicative interaction helps us to articulate how interpretive agency can serve as a basis for mutual knowledge making among classroom participants and how such agency is constituted in and constructed by classroom discourse. Davidson would point out that each teacher and student brings to the class a unique set of *prior theories* that influence the *passing theory* or knowledge created among classroom participants. Prior theories are affected by a great number of factors including gender, race, social class, and previous experiences with education. The novelty of each communicative interaction is guaranteed by the different sets of prior theories that the participants bring to the interaction. In classroom discourse, disciplinary knowledge and cultural heritage are part of the prior theory participants bring to discussion. *Passing theory,* or on-the-spot interpretation, is the ongoing knowledge made during communicative interaction among participants who occupy tenable subject positions. Essentially, the process of working out meaning is passing theory, even though there is never a single expression of that passing theory that envelops all of the individuals' perceptions of a discourse event. Thus, interpretive agency, while it finds its source in the participants' prior experiences, is effected moment by moment in the discourse itself.

In chapter 1, we distinguished *agency* from *interpretive agency*. We established agency as the ability to influence class tasks and topics, as well as the ability to influence the choices that writers make, and interpretive agency as the bringing of one's prior theory to bear in the creation of passing theory with others. Overall, this chapter explores three important aspects of valuing students' interpretive agency in writing classes:

- contributing to students' agency in defining tasks and topics, and thus tapping students' prior theories about writing as part of the ongoing meaning making in the class
- requiring both teachers and students to embrace subjectivity as represented in their own sets of prior theory and as reflected in the diversity of passing theories that may emerge during, and as a result of, classroom interaction
- making it necessary to recognize ideological stances within one's own subjectivity that, if unacknowledged, may not only inhibit participants coming to a shared passing theory but also may affect the agency that students are able to assume as writers within a given classroom situation

To show how these aspects of interpretive agency appear in practice, we examine an excerpt from David's first-year writing class. We explore how the excerpt itself shows students' agency in discussing the viability of a student's proposed topic for a paper. We then look to interviews that Helen had with David and with two case study participants, Ann and Laura, in the class to uncover differences in their understandings of what developed from the interaction. Finally, we use conferences between David and two major players in the excerpt, T.J. and Mark, to tease out how differences in the participants' investment in the outcome of the discussion affected their expressions of agency. As we examine this excerpt from these three vantage points, issues of gender, race, and class emerge as factors in the participants' perceptions of what occurred. We also suggest how mutuality was limited by David's reluctance to reconceive his notion of what counts as disciplinary knowledge and by differences among students' interpretive agencies that affected T.J.'s willingness to recast the way in which he imagined his text could be developed.

The Excerpt

Our examination of the excerpt itself focuses mainly, but not solely, on issues of student empowerment and suggests how valuing students' interpretive agency in writing classes contributes to students' agency in defining tasks and topics. Empowerment, a common theme in composition pedagogy, has often been discussed in terms of the power students have in the writing classroom to define class tasks and topics, as well as to influence the choices that writers in the class (peers and selves) make. Such empowerment is less often discussed in terms of both agency and interpretive agency. The important difference between the two concepts is largely one of control. As we illustrated in chapters 2 and 3, agency can be controlled, at least to some extent, as teachers invite or fail to invite students to participate in new speech genres of classroom discourse and through course architecture. In contrast, interpretive agency cannot be controlled; it is impossible to prevent students from interpreting the ongoing business of the class in their own terms, even though it is clearly possible to limit their expressions of their interpretive agency. We argue that, although it is basically outside a teacher's direct control, interpretive agency should be looked upon as a crucial and, therefore, valuable factor in classroom meaning making that should be tapped rather than constrained. In the example that follows, David clearly encourages the expression of his students' interpretive agency by engaging them in speech patterns that demand their contributions to class discussion. However, the extent to which this engagement leads to students taking agency is less clear.

The scene for this exploration is David's first-year college writing class about midsemester. For this day, David had assigned three students to present oral topic proposals as a way to get the class to discuss what kinds of topics were likely to work well for their upcoming thesis-support papers. In an interview about this class session, David described his purpose as "trying to get them away from those huge topics like abortion and gun control—where they usually just go out and gather a bunch of sources that agree with their position" and trying to get them to "whittle down their topics to a sensible size." We join the class as the third student, T.J., begins presenting his proposal for class discussion.[2] In previous exchanges, David had been content to sit back, letting the students do most of the talking. Here, however, David takes an active part in discussing the feasibility of T.J.'s topic. The nature and degree of David's increased participation mark this excerpt as a potentially interesting site of negotiation of agency and meaning in this classroom.[3]

David: Let's move on to, who's our third today? T.J. Had you forgotten about talking to us, T.J?

T.J.: Yeah, I forgot.

David: Well, let's be generative, then. What are you thinking about doing?

T.J.: Well, my thesis statement is "Stereotypes have made it difficult for unemployed African American males to find suitable employment in the country of the United States."

David: Let's start by responding to this as a thesis-support topic. What do you think?

Mark: NOT. [some laughter]

David: Why not?

Mark: It seems to me that Afro-Americans are getting a better hand dealt. It's just that companies wouldn't want to show favoritism in hiring. [eight seconds of overlapped and inaudible follow-up by two other class members]

Craig: The thing about it is you can get through, I mean there's so many different viewpoints, and if you take it like Clarence Thomas did, it's affirmative action.

T.J.: Clarence Thomas was a sellout and, ah [then, turning to Mark to address his concern], I was gonna survey black males and their situations and I also have a tape from *60 Minutes* that shows how they treat whites different from blacks because there was a hidden camera in four different firms. So don't believe that about affirmative action, that it makes whites more [inaudible] than blacks.

Craig: No, I'm not saying that. I'm, the point here, I agree with you on your—

T.J.: —but what I'm saying is, I'm not saying that it makes it impossible but what I'm saying is, they do have a lot of stereotypes, so far the affirmative action is not happening with every firm.

T.J. continues for another minute discussing the impotence of affirmative action, until David, who has remained silent up to this point, interrupts.

David: Let me ask you a question, T.J. Do you think that *60 Minutes* or *20/20*, if they really set their mind to it, could get films or evidence that white males were discriminated against because of affirmative action?

T.J.: I don't know.

Carol: No, I don't. I think that maybe poor white Americans, or something like that, but I don't think that.

Suddenly, class discussion erupts, with several students talking at once. Again, David interrupts and begins telling what he identifies as a "personal story." He explains the MLA (Modern Language Association of America) job interviewing process in some detail and then launches into a story about how two women dominated the limited market for composition and rhetoric jobs in English departments the year that he finished his Ph.D. This excerpt picks up his long monologue turn just before T.J. interrupts him.

David: They [the two women] screened people out of the market. I still got a job, but one of my classmates who is a white male who didn't have as many publications as I did and didn't interview quite as well has been on the market for three years and still doesn't have a job. If you are a woman—

T.J.: —Would you say that's the result of affirmative action?
David: Absolutely.
T.J.: You're sure?
David: For a job at [name deleted] University, initially I looked like a marvelous match for it. I didn't get a preliminary interview, and I couldn't figure out why. My friend who was not as good a match but who is a woman got an interview—I found out later that they were only interviewing women.

T.J. then immediately counters with a personal story about how he was discriminated against.

T.J.: You see, that's a specific incident, let's talk about a personal story at Iowa State University. [David: yeah] I went to [name of national pizza chain deleted] just to become like a cook, you know, they were hiring. Okay, I got there and they told me how great I was in the interview and everything but that the position had already been filled. So one of my good friends went back there, who is white, he went 15 minutes after I did. This is *15 minutes* later and they told him, well fine, you can start on Monday. He took the job; this is Monday. Tuesday morning he called and told them he couldn't work there because something came up. Tuesday afternoon I went in and the job was filled again.
David: So whose story is right? Is affirmative action—
Craig: —That's what I'm saying, that's not affirmative action—
T.J.: —That's not affirmative action; that's stereotyping; that's prejudice.

This excerpt illustrates how David's exercise of agency as a teacher sets limits for the expression of his students' agency in defining the task but also invites them to express their interpretive agencies in the discussion of the viability of T.J.'s topic. David uses the control afforded him by his role as teacher to set goals and to manage the class discussion set in motion by those goals. David has determined that the purpose of this class discussion is to enable students to better understand what topics work well for thesis-support papers, a particular disciplinary genre, and he exercises discourse rights not used by any of the students. He sets up the task and immediately adjusts it when T.J. admits to being unprepared. He allots turns—asking both T.J. and Mark direct questions, tells a long story, and even calls for a conclusion about whose story is right—a move that few students would feel they had the authority to make. On one level, this excerpt simply illustrates that teachers have course design and discourse rights that students do not. On another level, the excerpt suggests that David also negotiates some agency with his students in the choice topics of class discussion. David exercises control in that he set the overall agenda for the class session and chose whole group discussion on this day, which guaranteed that he would have at least a silent influence on any knowledge made. However, David also surrendered some control of what would be discussed within that basic task in that he nominated three students, including T.J., to introduce topics for discussion and made a "two-response rule" that he was not allowed to respond substantively about the viability of the students' topics until at least two students had done so. Thus, within the parameters that David had set, his students had agency in that they nominated topics for discussion and responded directly to each other.

Despite David's exercise of considerable teacherly agency in setting up the task, he invites his students to express their interpretive agency much more freely than they could in a traditional classroom where discussion is typically dominated by the IRE pattern of interaction. In so doing, he implicitly acknowledges the value of students' prior theories to learning. For example, after David's initial prompts, the students engage in cross-talk—reacting to what other students say rather than waiting for David to respond. Also, the talk in this excerpt is characterized by interruption. Although the instructor benignly evaluates T.J.'s first response, "Yeah, I forgot," he does so by essentially interrupting the IRE pattern. David's evaluative move initiates rather than evaluates, and it solicits brainstorming. Similarly, the next exchange sees David again substituting initiation for evaluation when he asks, "What do you think?" His "Why not?" continues the interruptive pattern. Not only is the IRE pattern itself interrupted, but responses themselves are also interrupted by other responses as the discussion progresses. Both the disruption of the IRE sequence and the clear invitation for students to engage in cross-talk suggests that interpretive agency is valued in this classroom. It also suggests that students have the opportunity to affect the passing theory developing in the class and that students' participation influences what gets counted as knowledge in the discussion.

This analysis illustrates that getting expressions of students' interpretive agency on the table is an important first step in creating mutuality, but it doesn't guarantee that students and teachers will embrace the subjective nature of knowing or recognize the inherent ideology that is bound up in their own and others' perspectives. In one sense, then, the conflict in this example could be read simply as David and T.J. having different prior theories about what kinds of thesis statements would be manageable for the writing assignment. David saw T.J.'s topic as unwieldy, and T.J. saw it as easily provable given his personal experience. In another sense, though, the excerpt also suggests that this discussion forced the class to face the subjective nature of knowing and that none of the participants had an objective standpoint from which to speak. In retrospect, it also seems clear that these differing subjectivities are ideologically located in the race and gender of the participants and yet these differences were not publicly acknowledged. The excerpt thus illustrates that even when teachers are not actively seeking to bring ideological issues into conflict, eschewing traditional patterns of interaction in discussion can lead to interactions where students' investment is very high and to exchanges which teachers cannot predict, control, or perhaps even fully understand in the heat of the moment. Teachers who attempt to engage their students in pedagogies that strive for mutuality must be ready to accept that there may be unresolved conflicts and expressions of interpretive agency that confuse, even baffle them at times.

In the next two sections we move to more detailed analyses that help uncover interpretive agencies at work. These analyses provide insight into how various participants in the class employed their own interpretive agencies and into similarities and differences in the versions of the passing theory that each saw developing. Although teachers normally do not have access to such information as they participate turn by turn in class discussions, examining these subsequent accounts allows us to flesh out the picture of interpretive agency that we have been sketching and to illustrate how class discussions may be usefully extended in subsequent interactions with students. Indeed, the issue of the suitability of T.J.'s topic is not settled until his conference with David two days later, and the way it was settled raises interesting issues about the power of interpretive agency to influence the actions of teacher and student alike.

The Interviews

Our discussion of the follow-up interviews between Helen and case study participants Ann and Laura provides insight into what embracing interpretive agency entails. Valuing interpretive agency in the classroom means embracing subjectivity in two senses of that word. In a general sense, classroom participants must embrace subjectivity by accepting that neutral, unmotivated stances are impossible. Every contribution to discourse by every contributor is motivated, whether that motivation is recognized and acknowledged or not (see Foucault, in Bizzell and Herzberg, 1145–48). In addition, classroom participants must embrace the subjectivity that is constituted by the unique nature of each individual's past experiences, which results in the prior theories each brings to the classroom. Valuing students' interpretive agency in classroom discourse thus becomes a means of trying to enable interconnections between individual subjectivities and disciplinary knowledge so that new passing theories develop. These new passing theories about disciplinary knowledge in turn become part of individuals' prior theories in future interactions.

This dual, intertwined notion of subjectivity runs contrary to a fundamental value in higher education: that knowledge is somehow universal and transcendent and that teachers and students should aspire to the objectivity that disciplinary knowledge supposedly represents. Thus, valuing subjectivity rather than objectivity raises its own set of problems. For example, it can be difficult for students to recognize and deal with the ways in which their own subjectivities affect their ability to construct shared passing theories with others. Students may avoid acknowledging that race, ethnicity, class, gender, or sexual orientation informs a situation to avoid being implicated themselves. It may be difficult for students to accept the fact that their own responses also entail ideological positions. As Pamela L. Caughie points out, students may resist knowing something about a text or a situation out of a sense of self-protection. However, as we will see, it may be even more difficult for teachers to accept the fact that their subjectivities are involved in their responses, because this view runs contrary to the traditional understanding of a teacher as someone who remains above the fray. Such acceptance also runs counter to conventional disciplinary practice that, since Aristotle, has favored logical rather than personally invested argument.

Caughie further suggests that it is important to ask not only "Who speaks and from what position?" but also "What authority is at stake and at risk?" (792). If we ask Caughie's question in terms of our excerpt, we might inquire what is at stake for Ann and Laura as white women if David's assertions are true? What is at stake for T.J. as an African American male if David's story is accurate? What is at stake for Mark as a white male if David's story is generalizable to his own situation? And, for that matter, what is at stake for David, if gender bias isn't the key factor that he feels it to be in his narrative? In addressing such questions, we turn to the responses of students from David's class. The responses of Ann and Laura illustrate how embracing subjectivity inherently entails differences in passing theories of classroom interaction due to students coming to these situations with their own sets of prior theory. The responses also suggest how gender can play an unacknowledged role in the passing theory that developed. David's response, immediately below, suggests how David's prior theories about his role as a teacher defined what was at stake for him in the classroom interaction and influenced the nature of his participation.

David's Perspective

David's interpretation of the excerpt reveals two somewhat conflicting aspects of his prior theory about his role in the classroom. First, although it is clear that he values expressions of his students' interpretive agencies, he sees himself as exercising a different kind of agency than his students do in class discussions. Second, his view of his role in the discussion suggests that he thinks he can not only work to help his students see the subjective nature of knowing but also maintain a relatively detached objective stance that does not require him to explicitly recognize or acknowledge his own ideological stance.

When he listened to the excerpt during his interview with Helen a day after the class session, David admitted at the outset to being "afraid that a white-black thing was going to erupt," especially since the class's level of investment in the conversation seemed to him to be escalating.

David: Now Robert Brooke might have said that I should have trusted my students to work it out, and I imagine lots of people wouldn't have minded; Pat Bizzell would have liked to have seen that happen in her class. It wouldn't have bothered her if T.J. went out of the room a little bit mad at Mark and Mark going out of the room mad at T.J.

Helen: Because Mark made that statement "NOT" after T.J.'s thesis [that affirmative action was not working for black males]?

David: Yeah, but I don't like confrontation personally, and I don't want my class conducted that way. So for good or ill, I stepped in with a story.

In other words, David felt compelled to respond to affective cues that haven't been captured in the transcript—a change in the level of emotional involvement in the discussion and a change in the nature of the interaction from consensus building to confrontation—and chose to do so by telling a long personal story.

In retrospect, however, David worried that T.J. might think, on the basis of this story, that David didn't believe that T.J.'s story was true or that it represented a problem. He said: "And it absolutely is a problem, a big problem. And his thesis was just too big." As David further analyzes his contribution, he contrasts it to Laura's.

David: Well, I guess I shouldn't berate myself too much for not being able to figure out exactly what I should have said, because who says I'm the one who's supposed to find all the answers in the classroom. Laura made a wonderful point that affirmative action didn't apply to T.J.'s situation, which is probably a more substantive point for him to deal with in terms of his thesis than my point was. It's interesting that she didn't need a five-minute-long story to do it. That always bugs me afterwards. When I left class I knew I had gone into too many details. I don't know.

Helen: But do you think it might have been . . . you said the level of investment in the topic was high and escalating. Don't you think that you had a little investment in the topic that was [2-second pause]

David: I didn't feel emotional about it, but I wonder if people would have seen me as responding emotionally.

David's view of his subjectivity as a teacher is further defined here. Clearly, David sees himself as responsible for monitoring and maintaining the affective climate of the classroom (nonconfrontational being his preference), as well as for certain course content (in this case, how to define a manageable topic). He identifies both these agendas as factors prompting his personal story. At the same time, he doesn't see himself as the only "storyteller" in the class or as the sole repository of classroom answers. In this interview, he compliments Laura on both the substance and style of her contribution.

David's interview reveals an underlying tension that valuing students' interpretive agency has introduced into David's classroom. David sees his students as having important contributions to make to the construction of knowledge in that he took active measures to engage them in the discussion. At the same time, David nevertheless sees himself, not the students, as ultimately responsible for classroom climate, despite his impulse to encourage his students to encounter each other in a class discussion replete with conflicting interpretations of disciplinary issues. He steps in with his story in an attempt to avoid confrontation between T.J. and Mark. In addition, there is no hint in David's discussion of this incident that he sees his own gender, race, or social class as affecting what he said. Although he values his students' subjectivities, he seems to see his own subjectivity only in terms of the role of a teacher, assuming that this role allows him to be both emotionally detached from the subject matter of the discussion and yet free to offer a personal experience. David's view of his role as an emotionally neutral participant (simply providing an example for the class to consider for its instructional value) fits well with what we see as the dominant view in writing pedagogy: teachers should be managers of conflict and certainly not involved. In Fishman and McCarthy's study, for example, Fishman's job as teacher is to remain detached—able to pose questions that bring students' ideological differences to the fore without threatening the social camaraderie of the class. The theoretical position that we have been developing calls these detached teacher roles into question: unless we as teachers are willing to acknowledge and account for how the ideological nature of our own prior theories affects the negotiation of passing theory in classroom discourse, then we can hardly expect our students to do so.

Ann's and Laura's Views

When Helen interviewed Ann and Laura,[4] they expressed no discomfort with David's invitations to the students to express their viewpoints in class discussion; they seemed to welcome this invitation to agency. However, both found David's role in the class discussion problematic; indeed, both disagreed with David's view of himself as neutral although they did so for different reasons.

Ann's and Laura's responses to David's decision to tell a personal story illustrate the interplay of students' expectations of the type of agency teachers should maintain and their empathy for the positions of various classroom participants, including David. First, both see David's role in this instance as subjective and emotionally motivated and as an unwelcome departure from his normal role. Second, both showed empathy regarding T.J's position. Although we do not feel free to establish a causal relationship, we suggest that this empathy might entail gender or, more specifically, students' standing as legally protected classes. Ann, Laura, and T.J. are all protected by affirmative action, either because of gender or race. David and Mark, as white males, do not enjoy that same status. However, gender does not completely explain differences in Ann's and Laura's interpretations of the excerpt: they differ not only in their reading of David's motives for telling his story but also in the extent to which they would have been willing to trust their classmates to deal with the conflict without David's intervention.

Ann has no doubts regarding David's purpose for telling his story; it was

Ann: Defense.

Helen: Really?

Ann: Yeah. He was defensive.

Helen: As a white male?

Ann: Yeah, I suppose, and just about affirmative action and stuff, mostly.

Helen: So you think he was defending affirmative action, or [two-second pause]

Ann: Uh, well, the student [T.J.], he was saying it [reverse discrimination] didn't exist, and David was saying, yes it does, you know, and to him [David] it was controversial, because he had an experience with it.

Earlier in her interview about this class, Ann confided to Helen that she was "kind of shocked" when David "actually voiced an opinion" and that she thought he was almost "jumping down the student's throat" in the process:

Helen: So his first, his first impulse was to say, yes, yes it [reverse discrimination] does exist, and this is my personal story about it to prove that. What do you think happened then to change that in your view, that purpose?

Ann: Well, I just felt like he was all of a sudden saying, yes, this is what's happening, and you're wrong, and I just think he said you're wrong. And then later I think he changed his mind and said, well, both occur, so let's just kind of drop the subject [laughs].

Ann interprets David's story as a substantive comment on the content of T.J.'s proposed paper and not as a ploy for showing T.J. that his topic was too large. She thus sees David "coming to his senses" later when he stops arguing his own point.

Laura, like Ann, sees David as changing his mind about halfway through the episode, but she perceives his initial purpose as instructive: "Well I think to see that T.J. was not going to prove his statement because it's not just in this one area. There's a wide, yeah, there's always an excuse. I don't know. I think it's a real dangerous topic [both Helen and Laura laugh]. Real touchy." Laura thinks it's okay for David to have shared an example from personal experience but suggests that he should not have pursued the story in such detail: "I think he [David] kind of lost track of what the purpose was in order to prove *his* point." Unlike Ann, then, Laura identifies that initial purpose as one of showing T.J. that he couldn't properly support such a broad topic but feels "it didn't turn out that way."

Helen: Are you talking about the way it sort of . . . at the end of the class period people really sort of seemed to get into it, started to get upset at least?

Laura: Some more than others [Helen laughs]. I think a lot of

people, students were [three-second silence] the instructor
lost sight there for a minute of the purpose, and it maybe
shouldn't happen, but it did happen, but he could have
handled it differently. But I'm sure that he probably left and
realized what he did [laughs, then Helen laughs]. He kind
of left and maybe kicked himself, but, I don't know, he's
human [both laugh]. It happens.

Laura is quite insistent on this particular interpretation, even
when Helen suggests another possibility. After Laura explains, "T.J.
is hard to convince of anything, and that's been his pattern through
the whole semester," Helen asks whether David, "knowing that pattern, was trying to be extra persuasive?" Laura responds, "No, I
think he lost track of his purpose [both laugh]. No, no. He got side-
tracked."

The differences between Ann's and Laura's interpretations may
indicate differences in each woman's prior theory. Ann's interpretation involves, in part, her reaction to David's apparent, and for her
unwelcome, departure from his past procedure and stance. Ann
makes it clear from the outset that she has "no problem" with David
telling a personal story, "but usually you think of a teacher as a mediator." Ann's surprise at David's response, then, rests not only on
her earlier observation that David seems to be taking a different role
than usual, but also on her prior theory that a teacher as a mediator
should remain above the fray. In short, Ann was unpleasantly surprised by David's actions.

Ann's expectations concerning how teachers should act seem,
in part, to be predicated on a prior faith in students' abilities to
work out difference through discourse. This faith emerges when she
suggests how David could have handled the situation differently.

Ann: I think in this case he [David] should have talked less,
　　because I'm sure that someone else would have voiced that
　　opinion, but [three-second silence]
Helen: You think so?
Ann: Yeah. I mean eventually one of the students would have,

I mean, maybe it's wrong for me to think this, but it would have been more okay for students to voice their opinions like that, one-sided, than for him, because he's supposed to be a mediator.

Helen: Uh-huh. So you think that the point would come out in any case? What about the students' contributions? How was that valued? Or how would you relate it to the class as a whole?

Ann: They, we were all kind of keyed up on this issue. They were brought up [four-second silence] I'm sure that they probably had their own experiences to actually relate to that, but when he gave his opinion, then uh, I mean everybody kind of looks up to him, because he's supposed to be the authority, more or less, so when we walked out of the room, I think most of the kids thought that well, the way I view it is David's way.

Ann's picture of what a teacher is supposed to be essentially matches the role David claims to have had in mind. It does not match, of course, Ann's perception of David's handling of events.

Like Ann, Laura sees David's response as devoted to promoting his own perspective and, as such, as a departure from his previous class contributions. However, she is not really upset by the instructor's handling of events. Certain topics, after all, are "dangerous," and teachers are "human." Laura's interpretation suggests that she sees a teacher's authority as resting finally on the instructional effectiveness of his contributions. For Laura that authority does not seem to require personal distance, as long as instructional purposes are not forgotten. In contrast to Ann, Laura does not view teachers as "above it all," but sees them as decidedly down-to-earth, as "kicking themselves" after making a pretty obvious mistake. And she counts David's pursuit of his own personal story as one such mistake. This difference explains why Ann sees David as "coming to his senses" when he drops his argument late in the episode, while Laura sees David as "losing it" at roughly the same juncture. Laura also sees students as capable of responsible action in the classroom, although in her interview she seems less confident of students always coming up with a helpful response than does Ann.

This examination of David's, Ann's, and Laura's interpretations of the excerpt illustrates three important points about embracing subjectivity in the classroom. First, giving up the notion of objectivity in the making and presenting of knowledge may expose teachers as motivated and perhaps, at times, even emotional participants in knowledge making. Accepting this role for teachers may be difficult for both students and teachers. Second, the three interpretations of this excerpt illustrate that the usual ideological terms of gender, race, and class serve as shorthand references to unique sets of prior experiences. These terms clearly have descriptive value but must never be seen as the totality of a given person's experiences or potential for contributions to knowledge making. For example, Ann's and Laura's differing interpretations of David's story tease out differences in their expectations of teachers' and students' roles in classroom discourse as well as different understandings of David's purpose for telling the story. Yet, it is also notable that neither seemed to see David's encounter with affirmative action as problematic. We might speculate that, as women, both might be more upset if affirmative action were *not* working in the way David describes. At the same time, both voice sympathy for T.J.'s emotional reaction to *his* experience. For example, Laura explicitly validates T.J.'s anger, even though she also sees T.J.'s entrenched position as part of the problem David faced.

Laura: I don't know as he [T.J.] really probably cared [about my point about affirmative action]. You know, all he saw was he didn't get that job. He was kind of closed-minded, well not closed-minded, but he had that purpose. Very tunnel-like. Narrow. You know, he had his sights set on something.
Helen: And he was, I think, angry, wasn't he? [Laura: Yeah.] about the situation?
Laura: Yeah, and I can't say that I blame him either [Helen:

Yeah]. [three-second silence] But, I almost think he handled it [laughs, then Helen laughs] better than David.

In this case, Laura's gender may have enabled her to empathize with
T.J.'s anger that was clearly based on a racially motivated incident.
In the next section, we will see that this link between gender and
race did not work to help T.J. appreciate the point that Laura made
about his thesis. Thus, we must remember that such concepts of
gender and race are never simple predictors of action or attitude.

A third point that arose in our discussion of these three interpretations of David's decision to tell a personal story is that conflict
can have real value in classroom discourse. In our example, the
value of conflict might be seen in the fact that it helped reveal the
reason for T.J.'s outrage, which did not become apparent until he
responded in kind to David's personal story. Yet, as Fishman and
McCarthy argue, conflict can quickly become unproductive when
students are simply shouting their disagreements at each other (355).
Indeed, David's original motive for telling his story—"to cool things
down" is probably best read as an attempt to forestall a shouting
match. And we should note here that at least one student, Mark,
found his story successful in doing so: "[If David had not told his
story] I would have either just shut up or just sat there and got mad,
or I would have, I don't know, probably would have just sat there. I
would have wanted it to cool down too." However, if we are to
enjoy the benefits of the persistent critique that Gayatri Spivak
associates with such tension, then we must accept the potential
for conflict that increased student involvement brings (see Phillip
Sipiora and Janet Atwill's discussion of Spivak's position). In short,
then, teachers must walk a fine line, encouraging conflict that ex-
poses difficult and at times divisive issues without fanning the flames
of conflict simply for the sake of provoking conflict. In any case,
conflict comes with the territory; indeed, as we turn to Mark and
T.J.'s interpretations of this excerpt in the next section, we will see
that refusing to acknowledge and discuss the ideological differences
that underlie conflict may limit not only the extent to which shared

passing theories can be developed but also the extent to which students can take agency in their writing.

The Conferences

Both the excerpt and the interviews dramatize that engaging students' interpretive agencies actively in class discussion does not guarantee that a single shared passing theory will automatically result. In addition, in the interviews we found hints that gender might have been a factor in the difference between David's interpretation of his role in the excerpt and those of Ann and Laura. Information from the conferences provides a clearer picture of how embracing subjectivity alone is not enough and how culturally constructed differences can inhibit participants from coming to a shared passing theory in instructional settings. More specifically, we see how race seems to allow Mark and David to come to roughly the same passing theory about David's role in the excerpt despite differences in their political views about the topic at hand—affirmative action. In contrast, unacknowledged differences based on race seem to have kept David and T.J. from coming to a shared passing theory despite their basic agreement about the need for affirmative action programs. Further, the discussion in this section illustrates that failure to come to a shared passing theory can have serious consequences: in this case it meant that T.J. did not write his powerful story.

Mark and T.J. gave us their interpretations in conferences with David that occurred a day or two after the class session but which were scheduled prior to the episode in question. Although it is true that Mark and T.J.'s responses here are given to David himself rather than to Helen, both Mark and T.J. had not been shy with David concerning their opinions about the class. Reporting Mark and T.J.'s responses, although situated differently, gives us the chance to include their voices in this discussion, even though neither was a case study participant.[5]

Although David and Mark share the same race and gender, both were surprised to find themselves in agreement about the purpose of David's story because of their political differences. In his interview with Helen, David commented that Mark thinks of David as "some left-wing liberal who will never agree with him on anything." By this point in the semester, David and Mark had already worked through several tense one-to-one interactions. For example, Mark confronted David after class the first time David passed back graded papers, amazed that David could give his paper only a C+. Because of these interactions, David reacts with friendly astonishment when Mark compliments him on his use of the personal story:

David: Oh really? You were proud of me? [Mark laughs] I was going to ask if you thought that [telling the story] was a good thing for me to do.
Mark: Yeah. It could have got out of hand.

Both David and Mark see the story as an attempt to "cool things down."

Mark is glad David interrupted with the personal story, in part because he doesn't have faith in other students' ability to handle the situation.

Mark: It was a good choice.
David: Yeah? Do you think that with the story that I told as an example, do you think that moved things along, or would it have been better if, if somebody else would have sort of been peacemaker?
Mark: Nobody would've, I don't think.
David: Yeah?
Mark: I think the story you told worked pretty good. After I thought about it, I didn't know if it was a true story, or if it [affirmative action] was actually blocking you, or what it was, the way you chose to say it. [David: Yeah?] It kind of made me stop to think for a second.

Like David, Mark clearly sees the situation as potentially explosive and the teacher as ultimately responsible for keeping the peace.

Mark's conference also reveals that he harbors some hostility toward T.J. and T.J.'s friend Pete (both of whom are African American). Mark states, "What burns me up is Pete and T.J. will put down or talk the whole class time about other people's papers, but the second when somebody says something negatory towards one of their papers, they say, or the class will just sit and listen to Pete and T.J.'s ideas." Mark has apparently been rankled not only by the past talk of the two, but also by the class's past tolerance of their discourse. Given this history, we suspect that Mark may have felt alienated both politically and, probably, racially from the respective major players in the episode. Mark seems only secondarily concerned with teacher and student roles; race is the more critical issue in the frustration that Mark expresses. Since Mark has constructed David as a political liberal, it is easy to imagine that Mark's approval of David's actions in this case, which could be interpreted as calling into question liberal and race-related policies such as affirmative action, involves a mixture of surprise and relief.

In sum, Mark's expression of interpretive agency and the limited agency that he took in this episode are not problematic for him because Mark is merely a commentator on another's writing project and because he has no particular investment in the outcome of the discussion. Similarly, Mark's own subjectivity and David's role as a teacher do not come into conflict largely because Mark and David share the same culturally marked ideological position even though their political views are quite different. David's discussion of this episode with T.J. is both markedly different from his interaction with Mark and yet surprisingly the same in some respects. T.J.'s investment as the writer of the proposed paper makes the match between expressions of interpretive agency and agency critical, yet T.J. and David's discussion does not crack the veneer of objectivity and the ideological differences between them remain unacknowledged.

In contrast to Mark's perception that David's story was both necessary and effective, T.J. sees it as basically irrelevant. This difference is particularly interesting because T.J. and David share the same gender and the same political views (particularly in that both support affirmative action). In this case, race seems to be the crucial issue. When David asks T.J. to evaluate the story, T.J. responds:

T.J.:   About interviewing women? I felt it was sort of relevant, but not really, because of stereotypes. Many women, not to the extent of rape, they have stereotypes somewhat. They get underpaid, because of this or that, but now they have it leveled out. Women vote. Men vote. The only thing that's not leveled out about is, some people say income, but I'm not exactly sure about that, so I couldn't say anything about that, but when you think about it, they're kind of leveled out. I mean, maybe women are pretty much considered equal. I mean, not the physical parts, but I mean the mental parts. That's stereotypically leveled out. I mean, it used to be like that. But now in today's generation, my generation, it's not really that big of a problem. I mean, I don't look at women as being any dumber or any smarter. They're just, the matter of sex.

David: There's so many issues here. Well, I felt sort of in the same position you did. It took me a long time [two-second silence] if I had been a black and a male, I would have been recruited more actively than the women were. It's not just black; it's any kind of minority.

T.J.:   Yeah, but then again, I can't really write a paper on an assumption like that, because if you said, they were kind of recruited more because they were women, black women were recruited more, unless, unless you had [two-second silence]

David: No, no, no. I had the same kind of proof you had from your story.

T.J.:   Ah, okay, yeah, because sometimes things are blatant and outlandish. I mean like what I did, what I went through. Sometimes they're just blatant and outlandish, and you know there's something. I mean, they're to the extent that you know there's no doubt. There might be some doubt, but like very little.

T.J. obviously sees his story as superior to David's, because his contained "blatant and outlandish" facts, which cannot be denied and which decidedly prove his point.

T.J.'s response to David's story in class and his interaction with David in their conference illustrates that the aspect of disciplinary knowledge is only a small part of what is driving T.J.'s interpretation. Ascendant seem to be prior theories regarding who has authority to speak to specific subjects. T.J. feels very comfortable challenging his teacher's authority, especially in the arena of affirmative action. For T.J., David's personal story wasn't particularly relevant because it didn't prove the point he, T.J., was trying to make. Moreover, David's idea that women are recruited more heavily than men doesn't hold water for T.J., because it's "just an assumption." T.J.'s argument seems to be that David, after all, doesn't know all the qualifications of the women that were being interviewed, so he doesn't really know whether women were being preferred for their credentials or for their gender. Apparently, T.J. sees a distinction between this and his situational context, where he personally knew the other person being interviewed and can, in his opinion, more safely argue that the only significant difference between them was their race. The fact that T.J. is an "A" student and that he comes from an upper-middle-class socioeconomic background might well have fueled his outrage that, rather than his personal qualifications and life experiences, race and race alone seems to have restricted his employment opportunities.

It is perhaps understandable, then, that T.J. sees the majority of the class as "closed-minded" about discrimination:

T.J.:   The only problem I saw with my paper was if people look at it in a closed-minded way, they're going to be just like that—no, no—no matter how much information I give and no matter how much I prove, they'll be like "Well, no, no, no, no," because if you stay closed-minded, people can come up with all kinds of facts and statistics just like the Ku Klux Klan.

T.J. perceives the class's responses (particularly Mark's) as stereo-typical and, as such, ultimately unimportant: "It was a general typi-cal response; [assuming that] any time a black wanted a job, all they'd have to do is put themselves in front of a guy and do half as good."

What is most interesting about T.J.'s interpretation is the au-thority that he takes in speaking to the racial bias underpinning his situation. T.J.'s assumption of authority provides an interesting gloss on his reluctance to admit a significant role in other students' mis-understandings regarding his topic.

David: Okay, and apparently you think that was the listener's fault, rather than your fault?

T.J.: No, I kind of think it was both. [David: Uh-huh] I blame it on myself because I really could *not* present all the infor-mation right away. But it was mostly, it was mostly their fault, because they went into it with a closed-minded atti-tude. That's like, if they would have read the thesis state-ment of the paper, they just went "no, no" and the paper would have been no good for them, because no matter how much I try to prove it, they just keep reading "whatever, whatever."

T.J. does admit to being partially at fault for the class's initial nega-tive response to his thesis in that he didn't have all the proof he needed to establish the truth of his position, but only after David directly questions him about it. At the same time, T.J. seems unwill-ing to really listen to class members' objections to find out what part of his case his classmates found wanting. The students, after all, are not operating from the same racial perspective and do not, in T.J.'s eyes, have his authority to speak on the subject.

Perhaps because of his specifically defined authority in these matters, T.J. does not see women as targets of discrimination. Al-though he acknowledges some possible economic inequities, he feels that women "have it [gender stereotyping] leveled out." He marginalizes women's experiences and dismisses their comments, although perhaps not with quite the vigor that he dismisses David's story. Although T.J.'s stance would not be considered by most to be the same kind of disciplinary authority that has formed the basis of teachers' traditional superior subjectivity, the authority that he draws for himself from his position as an African American who has experienced discrimination serves the same kind of distancing function for him. T.J. assumes an interpretive agency that is superior and unassailable by those without a similar knowledge base.

The failure of T.J. and David's discussion to penetrate the veneer of objectivity and address the fundamental ideological differences that informed their expressions of interpretive agency had real and unfortunate consequences in that they could not find a basis on which T.J. could take the agency necessary for him to write his paper on this important topic. On the surface, their different views of how their two stories would count as evidence in a paper seems to be the critical block to developing a shared passing theory that would allow T.J. to write his paper. When T.J. casts David's story as "an assumption," David insists "No, no, no. I had the same kind of proof you had from your story," and finally T.J. distinguishes his evidence as "blatant and outlandish." However, the real impasse seems to be that they do not expose the underlying values that block the formation of a common passing theory that would allow T.J. to write his story: David's commitment to a particular set of disciplinary conventions for writing and T.J.'s certainty that his experiences give him insight that those whom he perceived as not having experienced discrimination simply cannot understand. In the end, T.J. was not able or willing to see David's perspective, and David was unable to dismiss his disciplinary concerns and invite T.J. simply to write his powerful story in narrative form. Sadly, T.J. decided to scrap his story and write on another topic.

Should David Have Told His Story?

In this chapter, we have used a classroom excerpt, interviews, and conferences to examine the interplay of agency and interpretive agency, what it means to embrace subjectivity in knowledge making, and how all classroom participants' contributions must be seen as situated in their unique prior theories. In Davidson's terms, the students have constructed passing theories for David's personal story as well as for the class discussion surrounding that story. David also has his own passing theory concerning the episode, and not surprisingly, none of the resultant interpretations represent a perfect match. Indeed, the excerpt and interpretations illustrate that classroom discourse is subject to the interpretive agencies of all the participants. Accepting students as co-constructors of meaning greatly complicates our understanding of what agency and even "teaching" means. Agency becomes not only the ability to define tasks and topics, but also the willingness to embrace subjectivity as a key to learning and the ideological positioning that are inherent in this subjectivity. Diversity comes to define not only the ethnic, racial, gendered, and experiential makeup of any given class, but also the knowledge being made by classroom participants at any given point in the process. Teaching becomes a way of both interrogating the learning process as well as a way of negotiating the subjectivities represented in the various interpretive agencies of classroom participants.

We must accept that the effectiveness of David's story, as a classroom event, is by nature also open to interpretation. In one sense, what makes asking "Should David have told his story?" important is that it calls into question the assumption that a teacher's intervention is expected and necessary to making knowledge in the classroom. Asking the question also embodies the expectation that telling the story might be effective for some listeners and not for others. Asking the question also entails the realization that a teacher needs to have clearly established the stance that divergent interpretations are both expected and valued, to get students to take advantage of their power to make knowledge. A teacher who takes such a stance can still disagree with students' contributions but also must recognize that exercising that option may shut down student agency.[6]

We believe that the answer to the question of whether David

should have told his story is bound up in T.J.'s decision to drop his powerful topic and write on another subject. In one sense, David's decision to tell his story and his invitation to the class to express their interpretive agencies resulted in T.J.'s opting out of the opportunity to influence the thinking and actions of others. Because T.J. did not see his peers as having the authority to comment on his topic, and because he interpreted David's story as a counterthesis rather than as a comment on the size of his topic and the nature of his proofs, T.J. remained unconvinced that narrowing his topic and gathering additional proofs would address his audience's objections or, even, would be a worthwhile task. Certain of the subject as he understood it, he was resistant to adapting an expression of that understanding to his reader's needs. T.J.'s decision not to write about discrimination illustrates that actively engaging students as interpretive agents in classroom discourse does not guarantee the type of agency that involves influencing or changing events.

We also believe that the answer to the question of whether David should have told his story entails a redefinition on David's part of his subjectivity as a teacher. Reflecting later upon T.J.'s decision, David remarked in a conversation that he wished he had done more to validate the topic at the outset. After the completion of the course, David also realized that the validity of his story might have been compromised by his using it to make a disciplinary point. Although T.J.'s surety of his own position is likely part of the reason that he did not write on the topic that so clearly engaged him, we believe that David's insistence that T.J. fit his story into a thesis-support structure is an equally if not more important reason. Indeed, we believe that mutuality was limited in this situation by David's approach to disciplinary conventions at the time. Indeed, one of the most important lessons that this excerpt illustrates is that inviting students' interpretive agency may run counter to disciplinary genres, thus introducing possible double binds. David's understanding of "what topics and proofs will work and which will not" and of the students' need to restrict topics reflects his attempt to share his disciplinary expertise. But in trying to rescue his students from the silence associated with marginalized voices in the academy by teaching expectations of academic discourse, David inadvertently introduced another problem, a type of double-voicedness, into his classroom. On the one hand, his thesis-support assignment can be seen as in line with a postmodern teacher's role. That is, David's assignment might be seen as an attempt to "prompt the recognition and naming of used . . . discourse strategies" (see Donahue and Quandahl 13). By assigning a thesis-support paper, David has provided "what Foucault calls a 'counter-memory' foregrounding techniques [in this case, thesis-support organizational structures] as acquired strategies." On the other hand, David's assignment also may promote, whether David intended so or not, received patterns of argument, which are "based on revealing a single truth (a thesis) using all the available means of persuasion, [and which] run counter to new theories of socially constructed knowledge and social change" (see Donahue and Quandahl 13). In this respect, the assignment may actually discourage structures that would allow for multiple truths and stances. In so doing, it might even inhibit the type of multivoiced conversation David appears to value in class discussion (see Bridwell-Bowles 351). The assignment, designed to empower students by teaching them to "carry out those ritual activities that grant one entrance into a closed society" (Bartholomae, "Inventing," 162), also restricts students' opportunities to use alternative discourses, specifically alternative approaches to persuasion (see Lamb, Frey).

In view of such double binds, David's students may well come to echo feminist Karen Powers-Stubbs, who remarks with some irony on her own agency as a teacher: "I was the authority in the classroom only as long as I remained within prescribed boundaries" (in Eichhorn et al. 314). In this case, David's students could construct their own arguments only as long as they observed certain constraints. The irony of the situation deepens when we add to it David's position. It surely is ironic when David, and teachers like him, try to establish their own "difference" in an attempt to encourage students to "claim their own ground" but generate confusion, anger, or silence instead (see Karen Hayes in Eichhorn et al. 301–3). At the same time, as Lynn Bloom's personal teaching narrative suggests, it might also be that such uncertainty or silence serves as an important preliminary to student growth and action ("Teaching" 825).

The answer to the question of whether David should have told his story is, then, both "yes" and "no." The answer is clearly "yes" when this excerpt is considered as part of a larger pattern of inviting students to take an active role in the construction of knowledge. As the analysis in chapter 2 illustrates in greater detail, the interaction in this class session is a particularly intense moment in a larger pattern that broke out of default patterns of classroom discourse. When considered from the perspective of course architecture, as discussed in chapter 3, the answer is probably "no": David should not have used a personal story to enforce his view of a disciplinary value. If he intended to limit students' genre choices to expository types, then it seems unfair for him to use a story to make that point. Ultimately, then, the value of examining the excerpt, interviews, and conferences is threefold. First, it makes the possible complexity of engaging students' varied interpretive agencies apparent. Second, our analysis suggests that any excerpt of classroom discourse must be seen as part of a larger pattern of interaction and engagement of participants' subjectivities. Third, our analysis indicates that a willingness to embrace participants' subjectivities in knowledge making is not enough. This willingness must be accompanied by a self-reflexivity that explores a participant's interpretive agency for its ideological and cultural positioning. For real mutuality to develop, teachers must make consistent attempts to share authority over knowledge with students in all areas of a writing course, to enable an appreciation of the role subjectivity plays in knowledge making, and to acknowledge that this knowledge as passing theory will always entail the diversity and difference embodied in the prior theories of participants.

5 / Situating Mutuality and Transforming the Discipline

> By mapping the manifold ways in which authority defines people and relations of power—the discursive landscapes we and our students traverse—we can resurrect authority and make it more democratic, better suited to voices of both consensus *and* conflict.
>
> —Peter Mortensen and Gesa E. Kirsch, "On Authority in the Study of Writing"

> Yes, freshman composition is an unabashedly middle-class enterprise. . . . Indeed, students want and expect their work to be conducted in Standard English; their own concept of the language they should use reflects the linguistic standards of the communities in which they expect to live and work after earning their degrees.
>
> —Lynn Bloom, "Freshman Composition as a Middle-Class Enterprise"

> What avail is it to win prescribed amounts of information about geography and history, to win ability to read and write, if in the process the individual loses his soul; loses his appreciation of things worthwhile, of the values to which things are relative; if he loses desire to apply what he has learned and, above all, loses the ability to extract meaning from his future experiences as they occur?
>
> —John Dewey, "Experience and Education"

In this book, we have argued that mutuality is at the heart of alternative pedagogical practice. Further, we have described mutuality as depending on three factors: (1) reconstituting classroom speech genres to create reciprocity in knowledge making, (2) redesigning course architecture to bring students' experiences into contact with representations of disciplinary knowledge, and (3) valuing students' interpretive agency as a means of tapping students' unique subjectivities. Our claim in this chapter is that mutuality plays a crucial role in translating the postmodern understanding that knowledge is subjective and contingent into classroom practices. As a step toward transforming these practices, we discuss three issues that situate mutuality in current disciplinary conversations. First, like Mortensen and Kirsch in their epigraph, we see the need for a redefinition of authority, particularly how it is constructed in discursive relationships in the classroom and as it represents disciplinary knowledge. Second, like Lynn Bloom, we recognize literacy instruction as a sociocultural enterprise that can lead to both assimilation and resistance. Even so, we argue that focusing on mutuality leads to a new understanding of these terms. And third, like Dewey, we are concerned about the ends of instruction. Dewey's poignant epigraph asks us to consider the potential loss of student investment in learning and in social action that a singular focus on disciplinary facts can bring. In so doing, it underlines the importance of individual identity in education. A focus on mutuality provides a means for understanding how individual learning is neither completely independent of nor completely predetermined by social and cultural forces. Overall, we believe pedagogy that strives for mutuality is potentially transformative not only for the practices of teaching writing but also for the discipline of rhetoric and composition itself.

The Situatedness of Authority in Ongoing Discourses

In their epigraph, Mortensen and Kirsch situate authority both in existing relationships of power and in the "discursive landscapes we and our students traverse" (569). Students in writing classes continually struggle to attain authority in a landscape that features both the disciplinary discourse of rhetoric and composition and the local language of the classroom. Teachers in these same classes face the fact that authority is inscribed in cultural relations. Thus, even in classes striving for mutuality, authority for both students and teachers cannot be instantly redefined; definitions of authority continue to exist in the prior theories of participants. At the same time, student and teacher roles continue to exist only as they are negotiated on a turn-by-turn basis. As we illustrated in chapter 2, the speech genres that comprise talk in our classrooms can help or hinder students achieving voice and thus authority in the ongoing construction of disciplinary knowledge. Accepting a constructive view of knowledge and authority raises two important issues for the postmodern teacher: (1) how to represent the constructed and contingent nature of disciplinary knowledge without making it seem arbitrary or impenetrable and (2) how to invite students to tap their interpretive agencies—which is critical to the relevant reconstruction of disciplinary knowledge—without unfairly representing disciplinary knowledge as if "anything goes."

Mutuality assumes that students are in some measure immediately qualified to enter disciplinary debates and to assume authority in constructing disciplinary knowledge. In rhetoric and composition, the perspective that students are so qualified is not necessarily a vision shared by theorists in the discipline. Critics such as Patricia Bizzell have associated attaining such authority with being firmly situated in the discipline. In *Academic Discourse and Critical Consciousness,* Bizzell sees the individual's first step in entering a discipline as submission: "by entering a discipline, one commits oneself to looking at experience in the particular way established by that discipline." The next step involves achieving control, where disciplinary knowledge provides ways to name one's experience and to define areas of individual study. After control comes mastery, where "mature practitioners" in the discipline have the "responsibility of continually checking the community's activities against experience" and of, when necessary, arguing for change (148). Thus, mastery can lead to critical consciousness, which sees disciplinary life as rhetorical—as necessarily involving interaction with colleagues and dialogic truth. For Bizzell, submission to the discipline simultaneously gains a person a "liberating distance on experience" while fostering the need to "make a difference" in that discipline. Within Bizzell's framework, achieving authority becomes a matter of negotiating the tensions between individual preference and social con-

vention that are "inevitable in any community" (150). Authority is
clearly written by disciplinary discourses and is linked to disciplinary mastery. Those without such mastery are, at least to some degree, dependent on those who have it; students, for example, must
rely on teachers to grant them speaking rights. In addition, disciplinary knowledge can remain a fairly static entity—at least as it is
represented to students.

Representing another viewpoint, Gerald Graff accepts the idea
that knowledge is contingent, but he finesses the problem of authority
that such contingency brings by introducing a *counterauthority* in
the classroom. Graff's counterauthority is another teacher, who has
the institutional status to contest the presiding teacher's position.
This counterauthority helps the presiding teacher dramatize through
debate disciplinary knowledge making in action. While Graff's idea
reveals the contingent nature of knowledge to students, it also makes
them spectators rather than participants in knowledge making. As
such, Graff's approach reifies the traditional teacher-student power
relationship in which teachers have authority over knowledge and
students do not. Graff, in fact, sees the emergence of mutuality—
"*the destruction of this inequality* between teacher and student"—as
possible "only at the later stages of the process" of education when
students have gained enough disciplinary knowledge to join the debate (185). In this respect, Graff's approach echoes Bizzell's in that
a crucial factor in achieving authority is disciplinary mastery.

In contrast to Bizzell and Graff's approaches, pedagogies striving for mutuality both represent the ongoing, constructed nature
of disciplinary knowledge and make student participation in the
reconstruction of such knowledge the norm. In such pedagogy,
teachers must then find concrete ways to share authority over the
continual reconstruction of disciplinary knowledge with their students. As we've shown in chapters 2 and 3, classroom speech genres
and course architectures can provide concrete ways of bringing
authority to students' expressions of interpretive agency in knowledge making. Even so, teachers and students still face the problem
of negotiating authority in this setting where authority does not
necessarily rely exclusively on disciplinary mastery or on preestab-

lished cultural relations of power. Thus, pedagogy that strives for mutuality faces the additional problem of assigning value to the knowledge that is being constructed. If disciplinary knowledge exists only as it is reconstructed in the discursive landscape of the classroom, then there is no received interpretation that exists to provide an immediate and stable read on conflicting perspectives. As a result, reconstructions of disciplinary knowledge are contested to the extent that classroom participants' individual interpretive agencies are engaged. And conflict becomes an inherent part of learning. Although conflict will not likely dominate classroom interaction, teachers and students must not only expect it in classrooms striving for mutuality, but also must see it as an opportunity both to make the differences in people's prior theories apparent and to negotiate the relevance of such difference to the passing theories (re)constructing disciplinary knowledge.

In their epigraph, Mortensen and Kirsch ask how authority in the classroom can be restructured so it is "better suited to voices of both consensus *and* conflict." In so doing, they assume the value of having both consensus and conflict in the classroom. In the past ten years, many voices in rhetoric and composition have, in fact, similarly called for a new understanding of the potential value of conflict. John Trimbur has argued the *dissensus* can be as important as or more important than *consensus*. Gayatri Spivak suggests that crisis can have positive effects (in Phillip Sipiora and Janet Atwill 296), and Dale Bauer has pointed out that the "classroom is always a site of conflict" and will be "a site of conflict for both the traditional as well as the nontraditional teacher" (136–7). Indeed, a number of feminists have thus questioned "those pedagogical models which privilege only an atmosphere of safety or a completely maternal climate" (Eichhorn et. al. 299; see also Flynn 423; Jarratt 113).

These new understandings of the potential value of conflict still run counter to common expectations of classroom practice. Many composition pedagogies that embody the tension between a teacher's need to represent disciplinary knowledge and the need to enable a learning environment where students' contributions count as knowledge still see the classroom as a nonconfrontational place. For example, while Fishman and McCarthy invite divergent interpretations by students, their cooperative inquiry also strives to be nonconfrontational. In fact, they suggest that teacher intervention in class discussions can successfully abort confrontation and redirect discussion "to potentially more productive ground" (344, 355). Such approaches try to create classes that function as a version of what Mary Louise Pratt calls *safe houses*. Safe houses are "social and intellectual spaces where groups can constitute themselves as horizontal and homogeneous, sovereign communities with high degrees of trust, shared understandings, temporary protection from legacies of oppression" (40). Certainly, pedagogies that strive for mutuality may often function as safe houses. But pedagogy that actively engages classroom participants' interpretive agencies may also function as Pratt's *contact zone*. Contact zones are "social spaces where cultures meet, clash, and grapple with each other, often in the contexts of highly asymmetrical relations of power" (34). Thus, teachers who strive for mutuality must not only anticipate conflict as one of the many possible consequences of their pedagogy but also accept that power relationships may, at best, be fluid as classroom participants negotiate what counts for knowledge and who does the counting.

Literacy Instruction, Assimilation, and Resistance

Accepting the contingent nature of knowledge and knowing also raises another issue of authority: on what basis do we seek to change students? If, as postmodernism leads us to believe, there is no truth, then how can those of us involved in higher education justify our attempts to transform students? For more than twenty years, the primary answer to this question for rhetoric and composition has been variations of Mina Shaughnessy's pragmatic position, namely, controlling the discourse practices valued by those in power is a survival skill that students must master if they hope to succeed in the world of middle-class work. Indeed, Bloom's epigraph echoes Shaughnessy's position by implicitly identifying the expectations of dominant culture and of academic discourse as critical in defining the voices that students can develop as a result of literacy instruction. This perspective finds it reasonable to ask students to assimilate to the discourse practices valued in the academy and the culture because it is in the best economic interest of our students. However, pedagogy that makes mutuality its goal must ultimately reject this commonsense position because it too easily reduces education to the assimilation of students to a teacher's views of what they need to know and do.

Oddly, alternative pedagogy must also reject the most common alternative to the pragmatic position: that teachers have done their duty to students if they invite and enable them to critique the values of dominant culture. Such a position is one-dimensional in that it makes resistance the ultimate end of education. We have, instead, argued that resistance must be multifaceted if mutuality is to occur and that learning must be based on relevance. Even so, we must acknowledge that Shaughnessy and Bloom are right about the power of dominant culture. Dominant culture exerts powerful forces that cannot be ignored by either students or teachers. Pedagogy that pretends that students can write in any voice and any style without regard to others' perceptions and expectations is naive at best. Thus, the concept of mutuality, at least as we have defined it, demands pedagogy that explicitly recognizes the constructed and unstable nature of disciplinary knowledge and of cultural expectations, but, at the same time, entails pedagogy that values subjectivity. Admittedly, there is no magical secret that circumvents the knotty problem of how students' voices emerge from the interplay of their individual agencies and the cultural forces that seek to shape them. Indeed, the basis for intervention in students' lives becomes an ongoing commitment to relevance. This commitment requires that students' knowledges and experiences be brought together with disciplinary representations of knowledge, with the understanding that both are subject to change.

Given that mutuality exists only in this constant interplay, its ideological nature is largely dependent on the contributions of its current participants. Mutuality is thus ideological in a generative way. On the surface, this generative view might seem to co-opt the transformative agenda of critical and feminist pedagogies. Marxist pedagogy, for example, asserts that education necessarily reflects social class, gender, and race. As a result, teachers must realize and assume responsibility for the political nature of their practice. Feminist pedagogy recognizes that knowledge is transformative in different ways for different people, depending on how factors such as gender, race, and class are instantiated in the individual student. Pedagogy that strives for mutuality also recognizes that there are real limits on the extent to which a given teacher can enforce a political agenda without undermining reciprocity. At the same time, mutuality expects and accepts that some students who are privileged by their race, gender, or class may respond to transformative pedagogy by retreating further into privilege. Teachers committed to mutuality must respect such responses despite the nature of their own ideological agendas. Teachers and students alike must realize that mutuality begins in the expression of multiple subjectivities. Within this framework, resistance becomes not the end result of an ideology-based pedagogy, but an opportunity to negotiate knowledge and ideological difference.

As an approach to transformative pedagogy, mutuality is double-sided. On the one hand, it accepts the idea that pedagogy can and should embrace sociopolitical awareness as critical to our discipline's educational practice (see Bridwell-Bowles). On the other hand, it requires that such awareness emerge from the varied perspectives of the current participants in pedagogy. It also takes seriously Maxine Hairston's concern that ideological pedagogy can itself become a new and repressive model. Hairston criticized 1990s first-year college writing programs for too often putting "dogma before diversity, politics before craft, ideology before critical thinking, and the social goals of the teacher before the educational needs of the student" (180). Although critical and feminist theorists might see Hairston's criticism as leading to a dilution of cultural critique, we disagree, in spite of the vital role these discourses have played in the development of mutuality as a concept. We believe that pedagogy that strives for mutuality puts all representations of disciplinary knowledge—including those considered "traditional" or "standard" as well as those considered critical and feminist—up for active negotiation. Thus, assimilation and resistance take on new meanings. Assimilation becomes not merely a matter of acquiring received knowledge or submitting oneself to the dominant culture. It instead involves participating in the reconstruction of that knowledge and culture. Resistance becomes not merely a matter of critiquing the dominant culture using a particular sociopolitical lens (although this technique may certainly be useful at times). Resistance is situated at the intersection of disciplinary knowledge and the students' knowledge and experience, and becomes a matter of students' perceptions of the relevance of course readings, materials, and activities to the ongoing construction of knowledge in the classroom. This relevance, tied as it is to the multiple subjectivities and difference embodied in students' knowledge and experience, will be diversely defined and understood. In short, the choices for resistance will be many and part of the ongoing act of meaning making in the classroom. While we believe, then, that what students know about others' perspectives and cultures can be enhanced, we see classroom interaction, rather than direct instruction about social or cultural differences as the main vehicle of such enhancement for those striving for mutuality in their pedagogy.

Individual Identity

The contingent nature of knowledge and knowing also renders the concept of individual identity both complicated and critical. Dewey's striking epigraph at the beginning of this chapter highlights the need for each student to take away from education the means to continue learning. Dewey sees the goal of ensuring that students can "extract meaning from future experiences" as, at least potentially, in conflict with the goal of ensuring that students can "appreciate things worthwhile" (*Experience* 16). Although Dewey did not see the goals of teaching disciplinary knowledge and of fostering individual growth as necessarily in conflict, he clearly recognized that an emphasis on learning "prescribed" knowledge can result in the loss of an individual's "soul."

In the field of rhetoric and composition, the role of individual identity has been described in romantic terms, which portray the self as independent and inviolate. It has also been described in social constructivist terms, which portray the self as constructed by social and cultural practices. With the growing influence of postmodernism, composition theorists have, however, increasingly questioned how "individual" a student's agency can be. These theorists have also questioned how "authentic" a student's voice can be (see Ritchie). One of the most important contributions of postmodern theory to composition, in fact, has been to put to rest—at least in theory—the notion of the autonomous Cartesian self, which is able to create meaning ex nihilo. Patricia Donahue and Ellen Quandahl, for example, maintain that even student-centered pedagogies must require coupling the respect for students' ideas, experience, and dialects common in traditional student-centered pedagogies with the realization that the knowledge students have always involves society (12). Pedagogies that strive for mutuality do not "free" students by investing them with personal authority that is autonomous. Instead, such pedagogies enable agency by demonstrating that the choices students make and the freedoms they have are situated in social interaction. As such, students' agencies are "components of ideological systems" existing in the society (3). Some critics, however, have been quick to point out problems with locating agency in social interaction. Susan Hekman, for example, explains that accepting a postmodern socially constituted or constituting notion of self and rejecting the notion of an autonomous, Cartesian self is especially problematic for feminists because women have been placed in object position for so long. In short, giving up the possibility of autonomous agency might be doubly difficult for marginalized groups because it means giving up a status never held. Further, embracing one's inherent subjectivity might be particularly perilous in situations in which the contingent nature of knowledge is not explicitly acknowledged.

We see a clear parallel between the concern that feminists have in giving up the possibility of autonomous agency and asking students to engage in alternative pedagogy. Because students have not likely held subject positions in previously experienced classroom discourse practices, they might be understandably reluctant to embrace a constituted or constituting notion of knowledge making. Such a notion would preclude them from ever attaining the status of an autonomous knowledge maker that others pretend to have. Although debating the nature of the self is beyond the scope of this book, it is clear that pedagogies striving for mutuality must recognize an individual student's subjectivity as situated in cultural relations of power and as, itself, being continually reconstructed in our classrooms. Thus, one critical challenge faced by teachers striving for mutuality is enabling situations in which students must confront the ways in which cultural forces have contributed to the construction of their subjectivities. Students, in turn, must then recognize the ways that they can take agency in redefining their subjectivities where appropriate and desirable.

Recent theory in rhetoric and composition has begun to value subjectivity as a normal mode of operation for teachers and students in writing classes. Increasingly, subjectivity is not seen as the weak, emotional step-sister of objectivity but as an appropriate means of interaction. For example, some critics emphasize that bringing together people situated differently in and by culture is crucial to what Bizzell has termed critical consciousness. Jacqueline Jones Royster, who sees subjectivity as "everything," argues that using subject position as "a terministic screen in cross-boundary discourse" actually permits and enriches the interaction of perspectives. "Subjectivity as a defining value pays attention dynamically to context, ways of knowing, language abilities, and experience, and by doing so it has a consequent potential to deepen, broaden, and enrich our interpretive views in dynamic ways as well" (29). Indeed, the "politics of location" has raised numerous questions in the field about whether theorizing in the discipline involves transcending the personal or claiming it (see Kirsch and Ritchie 7). Valuing subjectivity has also led to redefinitions of literacy itself.

Deborah Brandt argues in *Literacy as Involvement: The Acts of Writers, Readers, and Texts* that the literate acts of reading and writing "must proceed with an awareness of the intersubjective undertalk that is carried in written language—undertalk that refers to the work of writing and reading and to the people that are involved right here, right now, with that work" (99–100). Indeed, we have argued in this book that interpretive agency is the intersubjective undertalk that informs the oral and written discourse in the composition classroom. Teachers and students who would achieve mutuality must proceed with an awareness of this undertalk. They also must have an appreciation for its value to the work of knowledge making and of writing, and to the classroom participants involved "right here" and "right now" in that work. Understanding that agency is situated in the "right here" and the "right now" encourages the idea that agency includes the ability to influence and interpret events both in and beyond the classroom. Agency is personal involvement in ongoing social conversations, no matter where these might occur. Or, to borrow language from Dewey, agency is soul.

Steps Toward Transformation

Throughout this book we have argued that pedagogy seeking mutuality must be transformative in nature. Both students and teachers must be open to transformation based on the new passing theories that develop in classroom talk. In a sense, we have argued that alternative pedagogy is transformative for those involved in each instance of its occurrence. Integral to this transformative view of pedagogy is a view of disciplinary knowledge as that which is continually up for negotiation. Unlike other views that recognize disciplinary knowledge as being redefined by experts, we see disciplinary knowledge as continually redefined by all classroom participants. We don't mean to suggest here that disciplinary knowledge that might emerge in any given classroom can magically change the discipline of rhetoric and composition as a whole. We realize that representations of disciplinary knowledge will continue to be shaped by powerful sociocultural forces such as academic journals, textbooks, and conferences. What we do mean to suggest is that the practice of alternative teaching gives pedagogy a seat at the table. In this sense, pedagogy that aggressively seeks mutuality becomes a force for transforming the discipline of rhetoric and composition.

The most important potential benefit of alternative pedagogy is breaking the binary relationship that too often exists between theory and practice. Because relevance is the key criterion in the continual reconstruction of knowledge within mutuality, alternative pedagogy by nature breaks down the usual divide between theory and practice. Granted, some might argue that because of this emphasis, alternative pedagogy simply "dumbs down" the curriculum. But this claim stands only if one is ready to accept that theory should be valued over practice. We are not ready. In fact, we see the interplay of theory and practice as one of the most important opportunities for learning. This interplay is where intersections of new knowledge and past experience occur. In a sense, then, the theory that we know how to practice is much more important than the theory that exists for theory's sake in scholarly books and journal articles.

Another way that focusing on mutuality in pedagogy is transformative for the discipline is that it depends on a view of students as motivated partners rather than as empty vessels or as underprepared or reluctant learners. A primary goal of such pedagogy is for students and teachers to understand their own subjectivities and to find voices that allow them to speak in the academy and other contexts that matter to them. Unfortunately, as Mike Rose reminds us, it is far too easy to read differences between academic expectations and students' knowledge and abilities as deficits on their part. It is far too easy to emphasize "the preservation of a discipline, not the intellectual development of young people" (197). Of course, students do have deficits in the sense that there are things they need to learn. The problem occurs when students are seen only in terms of deficits or when pedagogy leaves no room for students to participate in the construction of knowledge. Moreover, participation without agency does not necessarily lead to change. For this reason, it is important to remember that mutuality insists that all participants have "immediate membership" in the communities defined by the discursive landscapes being traversed.

A third transformative aspect of alternative pedagogy is that it leads to a different goal for education itself. Rather than moving all students toward speaking like television news anchors and writing like *New Yorker* essayists, literacy instruction should enable students to develop unique voices that allow them to participate in various conversations. As we have already argued, when mutuality is the goal, neither assimilation nor resistance can be taken as an a priori goal. If we hold to the redefinition of assimilation and resistance that mutuality suggests, change takes place as students and teachers alike adjust their prior theories to the passing theories about knowledge being constructed on an ongoing basis. Assimilation taking place in such a context ensures that learning and knowledge making themselves are not activities of acquisition and recall but of merger and extension. Resistance in this context ensures that learning and knowledge making are a currency whose value is determined by relevance.

How literacy instruction works in this framework can be seen, for example, in the issue of "standard" English. The notion that our students will be empowered if they learn standard English assumes assimilation in the traditional sense. However, assimilation in mutuality includes the realization that our students are empowered only if their input is valued in defining standards of language use in various situations and in constructing criteria for evaluating such use. An example of how this might work can be found in the way mutuality extends suggested reforms for the way professional communication is taught. If professional standards implicitly influence the content of our first-year courses, they explicitly dominate the content of professional writing courses. Courses in business and technical communication prepare students to succeed in professional environments where traditional rules of grammar and usage, as well as conventional structures for organizing various types of messages, are highly valued. Indeed, Carl Herndl believes that teachers of professional discourse who care about cultural change face a special challenge when addressing students in business and technical writing courses. These students characteristically see professional communication as a way of becoming "successful, productive members of professional communities" (350). Herndl recommends that teachers in these courses adopt a pedagogy of dissensus that allows students to explore the "sources of power and authority which condition their disciplinary and professional discourse" (361). Herndl's goal, which is in line with that of radical pedagogy, is to allow students to participate in academic and professional discourses "with a degree of self-reflexivity and ideological awareness necessary to resistance and cultural criticism" (361). In courses that strive for mutuality, teachers and students would extend that goal by using self-reflexivity and ideological awareness as aids for determining how individual writers can contribute to the ongoing understanding of what constitutes professional discourse and how these writers can adopt or adapt that understanding to specific situations. From this perspective the goal of literacy instruction cannot be to have students move toward a single view of what constitutes acceptable language practice. One goal might be to interrogate the interrelationship between disciplinary standards and views in the professional culture about acceptable language use.

Finally, we contend that alternative pedagogy is transformative for the discipline because, by definition, it is transformative for teachers. In this book, we have discussed how subjectivity is a crucial factor in student learning and should be valued as both a means of constructing disciplinary knowledge and a key to achieving voice. Here we remind ourselves that subjectivity is equally crucial to a teacher's learning and should be valued as such. Valuing subjectivity suggests that teachers should be reconstituted as an embodiment of a multiplicity of positions, languages, and desires. As Cheryl Johnson reminds us, teachers are written by the cultural identities that affect their students (417). In addition, Phyllis van Slyck sees the classroom itself as a place of "ideological becoming" where identities are always in dialogue and are, "like everything else, sites of context and negotiation, self-fashioning and fashioning" (168). What mutuality emphasizes is that our identities as teachers are also up for reconstruction. Valuing subjectivity asks teachers to recognize that their own standpoints as subjects are shaped by gender, race, class, and other socially defined identities and that these standpoints have powerful implications for their pedagogy (see Weiler 470). Valuing subjectivity also insists on the importance of teachers foregrounding their own positions as "subjects and objects of oppression" (see Wood 94). In the writing classroom, this might entail teachers situating themselves politically in the classroom, perhaps through personal narrative, and encouraging students in similar self-reflection. It would certainly entail teachers situating their teaching methodology and making explicit the ideology behind their approach.

Perhaps the most ironic thing about creating mutuality is that we as teachers are simultaneously the most potent force for implementing such pedagogy and its most likely impediment. Teachers of first-year composition and other college writing courses often feel overworked, underpaid, and undervalued at our institutions. Too many of us teach too many sections packed with too many students. Far too many of us do so on limited term appointments and without the benefits of tenure-track positions. Given these working conditions, it's easy to forget that teachers have enormous power to shape what happens in classrooms. Even though every teacher in the American educational system is to some extent constrained by curricular and programmatic expectations, the majority are relatively autonomous in the day-to-day functioning of their classes. In first-year composition programs, this autonomy may be largely due to the vast number of sections and to the fact that no one else wants to do the hard work of helping students develop voices that allow them to speak and write in academic contexts.

Although we cannot change dominant culture by a vote at NCTE or CCCC, we also cannot ignore the means for change that are at our disposal. Teachers of composition and writing program administrators have considerable impact on the college composition textbook and handbook market, for example. Traditional handbooks would become unmarketable if we insisted that textbooks in our classrooms made explicit the contingent and conventional nature of language rules and included examples of usage in varied registers and subcultures. In classrooms striving for mutuality, both a grammar handbook's discussion of comma splices and the teacher's concern that students understand how they are enfranchised or disadvantaged by dominant culture would have to be on the table for discussion and ultimately for resistance.

Our point here—and throughout this book—is that teachers' decisions about the kinds of speech genres that comprise class discussions, the amount of agency students are invited to take in the architecture of our courses, and the extent to which students' interpretive agency is valued (or devalued) are the most critical factors in implementing transformative pedagogy. As writing teachers, we must accept the real limitations of our situations (in the same way that all societal roles are constrained to some extent). But we must also accept responsibility for the power that our societal positions afford us and use that power to generate mutuality. And we must remember that none of the changes we have advocated in this book will occur unless we, as teachers, are willing to engage our students as genuine, if not in all ways equal, intellectual partners.

Notes

Bibliography

Index

Notes

1. Toward Mutuality in the Classroom: Classroom Speech Genres, Course Architecture, and Interpretive Agency

1. We prefer the term *alternative* rather than the more value-laden designations, such as feminist, Marxist, radical, or even critical, to indicate that our focus is less on why things are the way they are and more on what must be done otherwise (see McClaren). We understand that many readers will see the goal of mutuality that we feature in this book not as an "alternative" but as a goal they're already striving for. We use the term *alternative* to designate those pedagogies, regardless of label, that value and strive for mutuality as defined in this chapter.

2. Louis Althusser similarly identifies local and specific resistance, as opposed to global struggle, as making the "best sense" for effecting ideology-based change. Clifford adds that Althusser's distinction between ideology and ideologies "dramatically raises the importance of the apparently trivial conventions and rituals of teaching composition, for these same disciplinary behaviors help to install us as subjects within society" (42).

3. It is unclear whether Dewey saw this as a reasonable goal (see Prawat, Rorty for more on this debate).

4. In their study, Bellack and his colleagues discovered teachers' structure moves accounted for about 19 percent of the total turns taken and teachers' solicit moves, for about 30 percent, with students' responses accounting for about 26 percent, and teachers' reactions accounting for another 25 percent. Much like the IRF and IRE patterns identified later, this back-and-forth pattern, with the teacher making initiatory moves that control responses, the students responding, and the teacher subsequently reacting, allows students to comment on the topics nominated by teachers while according teachers control of the class.

5. Miller is openly using Mary Louise Pratt's concept of "contact zone" in his essay. Pratt defines the contact zone as a social place "where cultures meet, clash, and grapple with each other, often in contexts of highly asymmetrical relations of power" (34). We discuss Pratt's concept in more detail in chapter 5.

6. We thank a reviewer for this salient observation.

7. This has been famously described in Freire's "banking concept" of education.

8. Bakhtin variously explores this issue in "Discourse in the Novel" (354–55), "Speech Genres" (92–93), and "Notes" (145–47).

9. We understand that there are no guarantees. Merely because classroom talk is dialogic in the sense that we've been picturing in this chapter does not ensure that transformation will take place.

10. We thank Robert Brooke for his language here in describing the goals of chapter 5, as well as for his numerous other contributions to this book.

2. Toward Alternative Speech Genres for Classroom Discourse

1. It is not necessary to audiotape class sessions and transcribe the tapes to do these analyses. In his work with new teaching assistants, David often uses informal counts of turns during his observations or brief excerpts transcribed from audiotapes to help new teachers consider how the speech patterns in their classes support or undermine their teaching goals.

2. Because we wanted to make careful comparisons among the class sessions that we observed, we applied this coding system rigorously, carefully defining the terms and achieving a .80 agreement rate on a 20-percent subset of the data. However, the basic concepts that underlie this coding system—structuring, soliciting, responding, and reacting—can be used without such rigor as a tool to explore how teachers and students share authority.

3. Because we wanted to check the reliability of our judgments, we independently coded a 25-percent subset of the data and reached a direct agreement rate of .80.

3. Course Architecture and Mutuality in Student Writing

1. Dewey, of course, saw learning as starting with students' experience and continuing with the adoption or revision of certain habits, including the habits in writing choices that constituted disciplinary discourses.

2. Dewey's emphasis was on such continual re-creation. Dewey was not afraid to insist that education, while beginning with the student's experience, have as its goal disciplinary knowledge (or a collection of habits), which in turn constitutes a continuous weaving together of past and present (see *Later* 13:53; Russell 186).

3. Later in the course, David negotiated content knowledge more directly in a group project assignment in which each group of students was required to identify an issue they saw as important to writing, find sample texts to share with the class, and conduct a class session that used the texts to help their classmates better understand the issue.

4. This paragraph and a more detailed discussion of this student's work can be found in Helen's "A Tangled Web of Discourses: On Post-Process Pedagogy and Communicative Interaction" in *Post-Process Theory*, a collection edited by Thomas Kent (Southern Illinois University Press, 1999).

5. Students in Helen's class are given the option to have their assignments evaluated but not graded. This option is "renewable" with each set of assignments. Most classes that try the ungraded option like it, and continue to vote that their papers be ungraded.

6. *Teaching Against the Grain* is the title of Roger I. Simon's book about critical (Marxist) pedagogy.

4. Interpretive Agency and Mutuality in Classroom Knowledge Making: Or, Should David Have Told His Story?

1. To be sure, the issue of agency or authority within a postmodern framework is a sticky one. Because agency or authority here is so thoroughly situated, it is neither securely defined nor definable (see Bizzell, "Beyond Antifoundationalism" 665). This fluid or nontransferable nature of authority has led to disagreement among postmodern theorists regarding the place of individual authority within a socially situated framework. Social constructionists, for example, posit language as social practice and in the process seem to assume a normative social order that governs ethical choices. Social constructionism has met with resistance from those postmodernists who judge it as simply expedient. Pictures of agency thus differ within postmodern approaches, with some coming firmly down on the side of individual agency. Specifically, "externalists," including Davidson, see the writer as an individual (although socially constructed) agent, required to assume a strategic (ironic, parodic) attitude within the "circulation of discourse in society" (see Kent 84–91). Because externalism allows for individual authority in the construction of texts, and of rhetorical stances for that matter, it provides the impetus for seeing the subject as an individually accountable agent in a way that social constructionism does not. More to our point, such an approach allows for an enriched consideration of agency within social situatedness.

2. The names of the students are pseudonyms.

3. We recognize that in reporting this data we needed to be careful not to conflate our voices as teachers and researchers. Particularly, we did not want to privilege our post hoc interpretations as teachers over those of our students. For the analyses in this chapter, we took two steps to ensure this parity. First, Helen wrote summaries of each of the teacher and student interviews about this excerpt and drafted the gist of the analysis before David was allowed to see the data. (We had promised the students that David would not see their comments until after he had turned in final grades.) Then, as we refined the analysis of the

excerpt and jointly constructed the interpretive frame, we relied on the transcript of David's interview and Helen's initial summary of it to keep us honest in sorting out what were David's initial responses as a participant and teacher in the exchange and what were later interpretations of it as a researcher.

4. Ann and Laura were selected as case study participants on the basis of a first-day attitudinal survey, which was designed to indicate students' expectations regarding teacher and student roles in classroom learning. At the time, Ann was an 18-year-old first-year college student majoring in elementary education; Laura was a returning adult student majoring in business. Compared with their classmates' survey scores, Ann's score indicated a high initial preference for active student involvement, and Laura's score indicated an initial preference for teacher control.

5. Mark was a returning adult student just out of the army and majoring in animal ecology; T.J. was an 18-year-old pre-med student on a full-ride scholarship.

6. See our response (Ewald and Wallace, "Response") in the May 1995 *College Composition and Communication* for further observations on the teacher's stance taking in a classroom striving for mutuality in knowledge making.

Bibliography

Althusser, Louis. "Ideology and Ideological State Apparatuses." *Lenin and Philosophy and Other Essays*. Trans. Ben Brewster. New York: Monthly Review, 1971. 127–86.

Bakhtin, Mikhail M. "Discourse in the Novel." Trans. Caryl Emerson and Michael Holquist. *The Dialogic Imagination: Four Essays by M. M. Bakhtin*. Ed. Michael Holquist. Austin: U of Texas P, 1981. 259–422.

———. "From Notes Made in 1970–71." Trans. Vern W. McGee. *Speech Genres and Other Late Essays*. Ed. Caryl Emerson and Michael Holquist. Austin: U of Texas P, 1986. 132–58.

———. "The Problem of Speech Genres." Trans. Vern W. McGee. *Speech Genres and Other Late Essays*. Ed. Caryl Emerson and Michael Holquist. Austin: U of Texas P, 1986. 60–102.

Bartholomae, David. "Inventing the University." *When a Writer Can't Write*. Ed. Mike Rose. New York: Guilford, 1986. 134–65.

———. "Writing with Teachers: A Conversation with Peter Elbow." *College Composition and Communication* 46 (1995): 62–71.

Bauer, Dale M. "The Other 'F' Word: The Feminist in the Classroom." *College English* 52 (1990): 385–96.

Belenky, Mary Field, Blythe McVicker Clinchy, Nancy Rule Goldberger, and Jill Mattuck Tarule. *Women's Ways of Knowing: The Development of Self, Voice, and Mind*. New York: Basic, 1986.

Bellack, Arno A., Herbert M. Kliebard, Ronald T. Hyman, and Frank L. Smith. *The Language of the Classroom*. New York: Teachers College P, 1966.

Berlin, James. "Poststructuralism, Cultural Studies, and the Composition Classroom: Postmodern Theory in Practice." *Rhetoric Review* 11 (1992): 16–33.

———. *Rhetoric and Reality: Writing Instruction in American Colleges, 1900–1985*. Carbondale: Southern Illinois UP, 1987.

Bizzell, Patricia. *Academic Discourse and Critical Consciousness*. Pittsburgh: U of Pittsburgh P, 1992.

———. "Beyond Anti-foundationalism to Rhetorical Authority: Problems Defining 'Cultural Literacy.'" *College English* 52 (1990): 661–75.

Bleich, David. *The Double Perspective: Language, Literary, and Social Relations*. New York: Oxford UP, 1988.

———. "Sexism in Academic Styles of Learning." *Journal of Advanced Composition* 10 (1990): 231–47.

155

Bloom, Lynn Z. "Freshman Composition as a Middle-Class Enterprise." *College English* 58 (1996): 654–75.

———. "Teaching College English as a Woman." *College English* 54 (1992): 818–25.

Brady, Jeanne. "Critical Literacy, Feminism, and a Politics of Representation." *Politics of Liberation: Paths from Freire.* Ed. P. L. McLaren and C. Lankshear. New York: Routledge, 1994. 142–53.

Brandt, Deborah. *Literacy as Involvement: The Acts of Writers, Readers, and Texts.* Carbondale: Southern Illinois UP, 1990.

Bridwell-Bowles, Lillian. "Discourse and Diversity: Experimental Writing Within the Academy." *College Composition and Communication* 43 (1991): 349–68.

Caughie, Pamela L. " 'Not Entirely Strange, . . . Not Entirely Friendly': Passing and Pedagogy." *College English* 54 (1992): 775–93.

Cazden, Courtney. *Classroom Discourse: The Language of Teaching and Learning.* Portsmouth: Heineman, 1988.

Clifford, John. "The Subject of Discourse." *Contending with Words: Composition and Rhetoric in a Postmodern Age.* Ed. Patricia Harkin and John Schilb. New York: MLA, 1991. 38–51.

Davidson, Donald. "A Nice Derangement of Epitaphs." *Truth and Interpretation: Perspectives on the Philosophy of Donald Davidson.* Ed. Ernest Le Pore. New York: Blackwell, 1986. 433–46.

Dewey, John. *Democracy and Education.* 1916. New York: Free Press, 1967.

———. *Experience and Education.* New York: MacMillan, 1938.

———. *John Dewey: The Later Works, 1925–1953.* Ed. Jo Ann Boydston. 17 vols. Carbondale: Southern Illinois UP, 1981–1989.

Donahue, Patricia, and Ellen Quandahl, eds. *Reclaiming Pedagogy: The Rhetoric of the Classroom.* Carbondale: Southern Illinois UP, 1989.

Eichhorn, Jill, Sara Farris, Karen Hayes, Adriana Hernandez, Susan C. Jarratt, Karen Powers-Stubbs, Marian M. Sciachitano. "A Symposium on Feminist Experiences in the Composition Classroom." *College Composition and Communication* 43 (1992): 297–322.

Elbow, Peter. "Being a Writer vs. Being an Academic: A Conflict in Goals." *College Composition and Communication* 46 (1995): 72–83.

Ellsworth, Elizabeth. "Why Doesn't This Feel Empowering? Working Through the Repressive Myths of Critical Pedagogy." *Feminisms and Critical Pedagogy.* Ed. Carmen Luke and Jennifer Gore. New York: Routledge, 1992. 90–119.

Ewald, Helen Rothschild. "A Tangled Web of Discourses: On Post-Process Pedagogy and Communicative Interaction." *Post-Process Theory: New Directions for Composition Research.* Ed. Thomas Kent. Carbondale: Southern Illinois UP, 1999. 116–31.

Ewald, Helen Rothschild, and David L. Wallace. "Exploring Agency in Classroom Discourse or, Should David Have Told His Story?" *College Composition and Communication* 45 (1994): 342–68.

——. "Response." *College Composition and Communication* 46 (1995): 290–91.

Faigley, Lester. *Fragments of Rationality: Postmodernity and the Subject of Composition.* Pittsburgh: U of Pittsburgh P, 1992.

Fishman, Stephen M., and Lucille Parkinson McCarthy. "Teaching for Student Change: A Deweyan Alternative to Radical Pedagogy." *College Composition and Communication* 47 (1996): 342–66.

Flower, Linda. *Problem Solving Strategies for Writing.* 3rd ed. San Diego: Harcourt, 1989.

Flynn, Elizabeth A. "Composing as a Woman." *College Composition and Communication* 39 (1988): 423–35.

Foucault, Michel. "The Archaeology of Knowledge." *The Rhetorical Tradition: Readings from Classical Times to the Present.* Ed. Patricia Bizzell and Bruce Herzberg. Boston: Bedford, 1990. 1130–54.

Freire, Paulo. *Pedagogy of Hope.* Trans. Robert R. Barr. New York: Continuum, 1994.

——. *Pedagogy of the Oppressed.* Trans. Myra Bergman Ramos. New York: Continuum, 1995.

Frey, Olivia. "Beyond Literary Darwinism: Women's Voices and Critical Discourse." *College English* 52 (1990): 507–26.

Giroux, Henry A. *Border Crossings: Cultural Workers and the Politics of Education.* New York: Routledge, 1992.

——. "Living Dangerously: Identity Politics and the New Cultural Racism." *Between Borders: Pedagogy and the Politics of Cultural Studies.* Ed. Henry A. Giroux and Peter McClaren. New York: Routledge, 1994. 29–55.

Gore, Jennifer M. *The Struggle for Pedagogies: Critical and Feminist Discourses as Regimes of Truth.* New York: Routledge, 1993.

——. "What We Can Do for You! What *Can* 'We' Do for 'You'?: Struggling over Empowerment in Critical and Feminist Pedagogy." *Feminisms and Critical Pedagogy.* Ed. Carmen Luke and Jennifer Gore. New York: Routledge, 1992. 54–73.

Graff, Gerald. "A Pedagogy of Counterauthority, or the Bully/Wimp Syndrome." *Changing Classroom Practices.* Ed. David B. Downin. Urbana: NCTE, 1994. 179–93.

Grumet, Madeleine. *Bitter Milk.* Amherst: U of Massachusetts P, 1988.

Hairston, Maxine. "Diversity, Ideology, and Teaching Writing." *College Composition and Communication* 43 (1992): 179–92.

Hawisher, Gail E. and Cynthia L. Selfe. "The Rhetoric of Technology and the Electronic Writing Class." *College Composition and Communication* 42 (1991): 55–65.

Hekman, Susan J. *Gender and Knowledge: Elements of a Postmodern Feminism.* Boston: Northeastern UP, 1990.

Herndl, Carl G. "Teaching Discourse and Reproducing Culture: A Critique of Research and Pedagogy in Professional and Non-academic Writing." *College Composition and Communication* 44 (1993): 349–63.

Hollis, Karyn L. "Feminism in Writing Workshops: A New Pedagogy." *College Composition and Communication* 43 (1992): 340–48.

hooks, bell. *Talking Back: Thinking Feminist, Thinking Black.* Boston: South End, 1989.

———. *Teaching to Transgress: Education as the Practice of Freedom.* New York: Routledge, 1994.

Hull, Glynda, Mike Rose, Kay Losey Fraser, and Marisa Castellano. "Remediation as a Social Construct: Perspectives from an Analysis of Classroom Discourse." *College Composition and Communication* 42 (1991): 399–429.

Jarratt, Susan C. "Feminism and Composition: The Case for Conflict." *Contending with Words: Composition in a Postmodern Era.* Ed. Patricia Harkin and John Schilb. New York: MLA, 1991. 105–25.

Johnson, Cheryl L. "The Teacher as Racial/Gendered Subject." *College English* 56 (1994): 409–19.

Kent, Thomas. "Formalism, Social Construction, and the Problem of Interpretive Authority." *Professional Communication: The Social Perspective.* Ed. Nancy Roundy Blyler and Charlotte Thralls. Newbury Park: Sage, 1993. 79–91.

Kirsch, Gesa E., and Joy S. Ritchie. "Beyond the Personal: Theorizing a Politics of Location in Composition Research." *College Composition and Communication* 46 (1995): 7–29.

Lamb, Catherine E. "Beyond Argument in Feminist Composition." *College Composition and Communication* 42 (1991): 11–24.

Lather, Patti. "Post-Critical Pedagogies: A Feminist Reading." *Feminisms and Critical Pedagogy.* Ed. Carmen Luke and Jennifer Gore. New York: Routledge, 1992. 120–37.

Lemke, J. L. *Classroom and Communication of Science.* Final report of NSF/RISE, 1982. ERIC ED 222 346.

Locke, John. "An Essay Concerning Human Understanding," *The Locke Reader: Selections from the Works of John Locke.* Ed. John W. Yolton. Cambridge: Cambridge UP, 1977.

Luke, Carmen. "Feminist Politics in Radical Pedagogy." *Feminisms and Critical Pedagogy.* Ed. Carmen Luke and Jennifer Gore. New York: Routledge, 1992. 25–53.

Lynch, Dennis A., Diana George, and Marilyn M. Cooper. "Moments of Argument: Agonistic Inquiry and Confrontational Cooperation." *College Composition and Communication* 48 (1997): 61–85.

McClaren, Peter. "Multiculturalism and the Postmodern Critique: Toward a Pedagogy of Resistance and Transformation." *Between Borders: Pedagogy and the Politics of Cultural Studies*. Ed. Henry A. Giroux and Peter McClaren. New York: Routledge, 1994. 193–222.

Mehan, Hugh. *Learning Lessons: Social Organization in the Classroom*. Cambridge: Harvard UP, 1979.

Miller, Richard E. "Fault Lines in the Contact Zone." *College English* 56 (1994): 389–408.

Miller, Susan. *Textual Carnivals: The Politics of Composition*. Carbondale: Southern Illinois UP, 1991.

Minnich, Elizabeth Kamarck. *Transforming Knowledge*. Philadelphia: Temple UP, 1990.

Mortensen, Peter, and Gesa Kirsch. "On Authority in the Study of Writing." *College Composition and Communication* 44 (1993): 556–72.

Nystrand, Martin, and Adam Gamoran. "Instructional Discourse, Student Engagement, and Literature Achievement. *Research in the Teaching of English* 25 (1991): 261–90.

Pratt, Mary Louise. "Arts of the Contact Zone." *Profession 91* (1991): 33–40.

Prawat, Richard S. "Misreading Dewey: Reform, Projects, and the Language Game." *Educational Researcher* 24 (1995): 13–22.

Ritchie, Joy S. "Beginning Writers: Diverse Voices and Individual Identity." *College Composition and Communication* 40 (1989): 152–70.

Rorty, Richard. *Essays on Heidegger and Others*. Cambridge: Cambridge UP, 1991. Vol. 2. of *Philosophical Papers*.

Rose, Mike. *Lives on the Boundary: The Struggles and Achievements of America's Underprepared*. New York: Free, 1989.

Royster, Jacqueline Jones. "When the First Voice You Hear Is Not Your Own." *College Composition and Communication* 47 (1996): 29–40.

Russell, David R. "Vygotsky, Dewey, and Externalism: Beyond the Student/Discipline Dichotomy." *Journal of Advanced Composition* 13 (1993): 173–97.

Sarachild, K. "Consciousness-Raising: A Radical Weapon." *Feminist Revolution*. Redstockings of the Women's Liberations Movement. New York: Random, 1975.

Schniederwind, N. "Teaching Feminist Process." *Women's Studies Quarterly* 15 (1987): 15–31.

Segal, Judy. "Pedagogies of Decentering and a Discourse of Failure." *Rhetoric Review* 15 (1996): 174–91.

Shaughnessy, Mina P. *Errors and Expectations: A Guide for the Teacher of Basic Writing*. New York: Oxford UP, 1977.

Simon, Roger I. *Teaching Against the Grain*. New York: Bergin, 1992.

Sinclair, J. M., and R. M. Coulthard. *Towards an Analysis of Discourse: The English Used by Teachers and Pupils*. London: Oxford UP, 1975.

Sipiora, Phillip, and Janet Atwill. "Rhetoric and Cultural Explanation: A Discussion with Gayatri Charkravoty Spivak." *Journal of Advanced Composition* 10 (1990): 293–304.

Sommers, Jeffrey. "The Writer's Memo: Collaboration, Response, and Development." *Writing and Response: Theory, Practice, and Research.* Ed. Chris M. Anson. Urbana: NCTE, 1989. 174–86.

Todorov, Tzvetan. *Mikhail Bakhtin: The Dialogical Principle.* Trans. Wlad Godzich. Minneapolis: U of Minnesota P, 1984.

Tompkins, Jane. "Pedagogy of the Distressed." *College English* 52 (1990): 653–60.

Trimbur, John. "The Politics of Radical Pedagogy: A Plea for 'A Dose of Vulgar Marxism.'" *College English* 56 (1994): 194–206.

Tuana, Nancy, ed. *Feminism and Science.* Bloomington: Indiana UP, 1989.

van Slyck, Phyllis. "Repositioning Ourselves in the Contact Zone." *College English* 59 (1997): 149–70.

Villanueva, Victor, Jr., ed. *Cross-Talk in Composition Theory: A Reader.* Urbana: NCTE, 1997.

Wallace, David L., and Annissa Bell. "Being Black at a Predominantly White University." *College English* 61 (1999): 307–27.

Weedon, Chris. *Feminist Practice and Poststructuralist Theory.* Cambridge: Blackwell, 1987.

Weiler, Kathleen, ed. *Women Teaching for Change: Gender, Class, and Power.* South Hadley: Bergin, 1988.

Wood, Robert G. "The Dialectic Suppression of Feminist Thought in Radical Pedagogy." *Journal of Advanced Composition* 13 (1993): 79–95.

Yancey, Kathleen Blake. "Introduction: Definition, Intersection, and Difference—Mapping the Landscape of Voice." *Voices on Voice: Perspectives, Definitions, Inquiry.* Ed. Kathleen Blake Yancey. Urbana: NCTE, 1994. vii–xxiv.

Zawacki, Terry Myers. "Recomposing as a Woman—An Essay in Different Voices." *College Composition and Communication* 43 (1992): 32–38.

Index

161

DAVID L. WALLACE is an associate professor of rhetoric and composition in the Department of English at Iowa State University where he teaches first-year composition courses; undergraduate rhetorical history and theory courses; and graduate courses in research design, pedagogical theory, and the history of rhetoric. He has published articles in *College English, College Composition and Communication, JAC: Journal of Composition Theory,* and *Research in the Teaching of English.* He is currently working on a set of case studies that examine how gender, race, class, and sexual orientation affect the subjectivities that first-year college students take in classroom discourse and in their writing.

HELEN ROTHSCHILD EWALD is a professor of rhetoric and composition in the Department of English at Iowa State University where she teaches first-year honors composition; undergraduate rhetorical analysis and argumentative writing courses; and graduate courses in academic writing, pedagogical theory, and theory and research in professional communication. She has published articles in various journals, including *College Composition and Communication* and *JAC: Journal of Composition Theory.* She has also written a first-year composition textbook, *Writing as Process: Invention and Convention,* and coauthored a professional writing textbook, *Business Communication.* She is presently exploring issues of identity and community in the writing classroom.

Studies in Writing & Rhetoric

In 1980 the Conference on College Composition and Communication established the Studies in Writing & Rhetoric (SWR) series as a forum for monograph-length arguments or presentations that engage general compositionists. SWR encourages extended essays or research reports addressing any issue in composition and rhetoric from any theoretical or research perspective as long as the general significance to the field is clear. Previous SWR publications serve as models for prospective authors; in addition, contributors may propose alternate formats and agendas that inform or extend the field's current debates.

SWR is particularly interested in projects that connect the specific research site or theoretical framework to contemporary classroom and institutional contexts of direct concern to compositionists across the nation. Such connections may come from several approaches, including cultural, theoretical, field-based, gendered, historical, and interdisciplinary. SWR especially encourages monographs by scholars early in their careers, by established scholars who wish to share an insight or exhortation with the field, and by scholars of color.

The SWR series editor and editorial board members are committed to working closely with prospective authors and offering significant developmental advice for encouraged manuscripts and prospectuses. Editorships rotate every five years. Prospective authors intending to submit a prospectus during the 1997 to 2002 editorial appointment should obtain submission guidelines from Robert Brooke, SWR editor, University of Nebraska-Lincoln, Department of English, P.O. Box 880337, 202 Andrews Hall, Lincoln, NE 68588-0337.

General inquiries may also be addressed to Sponsoring Editor, Studies in Writing & Rhetoric, Southern Illinois University Press, P.O. Box 3697, Carbondale, IL 62902-3697.